Path of Emergence:
From Loss to Triumph

Sheena Eizmendiz

Cover Design: Visuapex Creatives
Photo Credit: Laboratorio1919
www.sheenaeizmendiz.com

Dedication

This book is for the women who remain in prison. The women who shared this journey with me, who became a true expression of support and friendship. These are our truths. To Lisa, Sylvia, Vicky, Aimee, Wanda, Daisy, Marietha, Isachi, Blanquita and so many others. It's because of you that I am strong enough to share both my losses, and yours. This book is our voice. The world will be inspired from hearing us.

Also, to those experiencing loss in any capacity, be it imprisonment or not. Prison isn't always a place you go to, it's a state of mind you live in. Loss is not the end. It truly is the catalyst for impenetrable growth, should you allow it to be.

Finally, I dedicate this book to my parents and my two daughters, Gemeny and Amber. Your unwavering love sustained me. I could not have done this alone. Your very own existence propelled me forward and continues to empower me today. I am deeply grateful and humbled.

Contents

Author's Note

This is a work of creative nonfiction. The events are
portrayed to the best of Sheena Eizmendiz's
memory. While all the stories in this book are true,
some names and identifying details have been
changed to protect the privacy of
the people involved.

ISBN: 978-0-9968446-0-4

Path

OF EMERGENCE

FROM LOSS TO TRIUMPH

Introduction

There is no doubt in my mind that our prison system is flawed. No doubt that I was screwed by the same system that disrupted my peace and changed my life forever. However, this book is not about that, this book is about truth, loss and how to emerge from having lost everything, including, losing yourself.

It took me a while to truly accept that none of us are victims of our circumstances, we are all participants. Unwittingly, we volunteer to endure certain experiences that will help us evolve as better humans. Even if at the moment none of it makes any sense.

Throughout my experience, I learned that every so-called, 'obstacle', is a step closer to our awakening. We are all equally a divine piece of our Creator, our God, your God, whomever, or, whatever that may be. Each one of us is here to learn something valuable, something purposeful.

This book does not claim to be the anecdote for freeing yourself from your ego or reaching what many call, enlightenment. It is simply an account of facts and personal experiences. It is my story - the story of loss and triumph, mental and physical imprisonment, spiritual liberation and redemption. I learned that trials were simply the soil in which growth stems from. It is with great excitement that I share with you the accounts which took place during a period of my life when I was stripped from everything I once knew. A time in my life when my world was flipped upside down. I get to share with you how a phoenix falls and rises from the ashes, but, not before having experienced enormous pain and sorrow. Not before having lost oneself to its own ego.

For me, it was discovering my true purpose in life. My journey was not in vain. It was brutal, but, it was purposeful. As humans, we tend to reflect on moments of deep transition, moments that leave us feeling lost and hopeless. During such times, we tend to unwisely blame others for the events that happen to us. Our world suddenly crumbles, and we're left fearing that our life will never be the same again. Shaken, we come to the resounding conclusion that life is only made up of pain.

Oftentimes we ask, why do people have to get sick? Why do we die? Why do we need to suffer? If our God designed a world out of love for His children, why didn't He create a world filled with only peace and joy? And yet in times of loss, when we are feeling hopeless and helpless, we are innately driven to seek God's assistance in healing our pain.

To me, the pain I endured was meaningful because of the changes it evoked in my personal life. I learned that the cause of our pain is relative. Even if we try to understand what the cause of our suffering is, we may never find it. Pain is a way for us to realize that something is wrong - whether it is physical or emotional. Pain is a messenger. It comes to tell us that something must change.

It's impossible to indefinitely neglect the source of our pain. Over time, we become stuck in a cycle of negative manifestation. The truth is, we can prevent many of the tragedies we experience. Granted, some are unavoidable and part of some divine plan, but, others are merely caused by a repeated thought or belief created by ourselves. Experiencing painful moments is one of the inevitable realities of life. Nonetheless, it is an astonishing and powerful process that begins with a mere thought. Ego-driven thoughts create pain and disarray. I found myself engrossed in those types of thoughts many times before, anxiously doubting the standstills. There were so many things I wanted to do but it seemed that the timing was not right. I had to sit and wait, learn and grow.

I decided to write this book out of my own need to express the things I have learned and now want to share. I write with the hopes to inspire, inform, and assist anyone in a tragic predicament of any kind.

This is a very personal book, compelled by a life-altering experience. All of the events in this book are real, though some of the names have been changed in order to protect and respect the characters' identities. These stories are intended to dissolve pragmatic ideals and imbalanced perceptions of life, spirituality, and our prison system. My intention is that you understand, accept and solve life's greatest teachings and that this book can be an instrument in your journey.

After having experienced what many would consider tragic, I realized how triumphant I was inside. It wasn't until I was deprived of the freedom I once knew, when I lost everything I knew as truth, when my life was literally uprooted, dismantled, and shaken, that I realized that there was only one thing I can control. I can only control the way I choose to define myself, my story's definition is up to me. The way I digest the situation, that is my only control. Accepting the roles I play in all of my circumstances. I am accountable for how I allow any of it to affect me. I create and co-create all things. This is the only real control I possess. This is my journey. I now want to share it with you.

In summary, this book documents my undoing, and my rebirth.

Chapter 1

April 18th, 2018

    I've been dreaming of this moment for nine months. I've been willing time forward, yearning for this day to come. Although it's spring here, and the weather is quite pleasant, it feels like my emotions are scorching. As if there is a forest fire that has been ignited inside of me. I'm being released today. Holy shit, I'm being released today! As I am saying this, I'm feeling torn. On the one hand, I am finally free, on the other, I am leaving the women who have sustained me throughout this tolling ordeal. Why do I get to leave but they can't? Why can't I take them with me? I feel hugely responsible for them. Feelings of guilt are eating me alive right now. I can't shake the feeling that I am leaving them behind. I hate myself for leaving them here. After they've loved and encouraged me, how can I walk away? My feet feel as though they are made of lead each step away from them weighs me down like anchors, leaving me short of breath. I feel like gasping for air. This is overwhelmingly bittersweet and downright painful. I want to rush out of these prison walls and scream at the top of my lungs, I'm free! I simultaneously want to scoop these women up and hold on tight.

the products, snacks, and people everywhere. I don't know where to begin. I glance down at my list of toiletries and begin to aimlessly walk down the aisles. I am mesmerized and silent. I have gone without Pringles, minty organic shampoo, and soft toilet paper for so long, I don't know how to process this influx of information and goods. I begin to chew on my lip. Time is passing, and I cannot find what I need. I am too nervous to ask an associate for help. I feel so out of place, like everybody knows I have just been released from a federal prison. I'm just going to turn on my heels and bolt out of the store with nothing in hand. I'm leaving everything in the cart. I can't do this today. I begin jogging, then sprinting towards the halfway house. I do not want to be late. I feel so exposed and all I want to do is curl up in my bed and close my eyes until everything is familiar again. I'm relearning everything, including how to cross the street.

I've realized that people walk and speak incredibly fast out here. People are constantly in a state of doing something. Prison allowed me to simply be; to operate from a constant state of being. No one was rushing anywhere. If I wanted to sleep, I could. If I wanted to read, I could. If I wanted to exercise, I could. There was no hurry. It was a calmer state of allowing. Out here, you're in a state of doing all the time. I'm realizing that you miss so much in this process. I look at people and think, what's wrong with you? Why do you have to do things that way? If prison taught me anything, it's that people out here aren't living, they are simply surviving through life. They're speed walking through their lives, in a constant progression from one chore to the next. To-do lists propel people forward, more so than passion and self-awareness. I wonder if I was like this before, even though I know I was.

Initially, I thought I was the broken one. Now I'm beginning to wonder if they're the ones who are broken. Prison taught me to honor each moment and to be in-tune with my feelings. It also taught me that we are all innately equal. That's not true out here. I see the distinctions, the judgments, and the assumptions. In prison however, we are all equal. There are no differentiators. We all wear the same clothes, shoes, and eat the same food. There are no lawyers, or thugs, or doctors - it's an equalized system. Out here, I realize the disparity amongst people. There is so much division. People are so anchored to their Facebook status', their belongings, and their credentials. In prison, we're each allowed $300 a month on commissary, regardless of how much money you may have in the outside world. That's the cap off. We are kept equal.

Readjusting to the world again has been a challenge these past few days. How do I incorporate these lessons and this newfound awareness while still trying to integrate myself? Does one deny the other? I spend a lot of time observing and reflecting.

I wonder if I will ever be me again. I don't even know if I truly want to go back to being the old me. I lived my life on a hamster wheel of sorts. Prison gave me the opportunity to reflect and evaluate the way I was living my life. As horrific as prison might be, there is a lot to learn from it if one allows oneself to.

I wish there was more support and resources from the halfway house. My counselor is so fucking incompetent. She is only here for a paycheck, nothing more. She offers no insight, no encouragement, and no direction. The men and women who live here at Riverside are just as daunted. We have to do this on our own. It's infuriating. Thankfully, I know enough to get by, but what of the men and women who have never known life outside of those prison walls? Who is helping and supporting them to make a successful and healthy transition back into society? How can they be expected to change their lives if they are not given the tools and the support to do so? We are cogs in an ever-growing machine. The men and women here have to fend for themselves. I've met several who have come from serving long sentences from different prisons around the country. I wonder how they must feel. This must be very difficult on them too. It pains me to imagine how lost they must be. Imagine for a second that you have spent the greater part of your life in prison. In a place where technology does not exist. Prison is so unevolved. You have no clue what's going on in the real world other than the rumors you hear or the little bit of news you catch on a day to day basis. These men and women have been thrown to the wolves. No one is guiding them. I feel helpless. I can't step in and help. I want to help them so badly, but I can't. I still need to help myself throughout all of this. I've always believed that in order to help others, we must come from a good place to do so and I'm not in a good place right now. There isn't much I can offer them, so, I can only sit and watch how broken the system is and do nothing. I can't stand to do nothing. A part of me wants to tell the counselors how inadequate they are for this job. I want to sit down and strategize with these incompetents to come up with a plan to help these people reintegrate into society. I have the skills that they don't have and it burns inside me to know that I can't control this situation. I have to stay quiet, for now.

I live in a crappy room with eight women who like me, were recently released from prison. Crowded is an understatement. At least our lockers are larger than the ones we had in prison. I'm one of the few who are allowed to stash some junk food because I'm hypoglycemic, otherwise, we aren't allowed to have any food in our rooms. All the women in my room came from different prisons. My old bunkie is here too. She is staying in my room. She looks a lot better out here than she did in prison. Damn, she even walks faster too. She looks empowered, or, at least she seems to be. I don't really associate with her much here, I did so in prison. I'm just counting the days to leave this place. I've made friends with one of the other women, her name is Yvette. She served three years at another camp a few hours from Coleman. Her jokes always make me laugh. She learned to crochet in prison and she now sells a lot of the outfits she makes. Like me, she is a bit rebellious. When she and I get together, we feel like we don't have to put up with anyone's crap in here.

Men live here too, but, we aren't allowed to speak to any of them. It's so childish. They eat with us, they even hang outside with us. They wash their clothes in the same laundry room as us, but somehow, we aren't allowed to speak to them. The guys are kind enough to start the washers and dryers for us so we don't have to pay to wash our clothes. We simply let them know when we are going to wash and one of them walks inside the laundry room and sticks a piece of metal in the coin hole until it turns on. We have to be careful that we aren't caught communicating. One of the guys is Yvette's brother, he was also involved in her case. Regardless of them being siblings, they are not allowed to speak to each other.

They should be paying more attention to our living conditions and not so much how and with whom we interact. For instance, It's storming really bad outside and there is water inside our room. There is rain running down the walls, out of the outlets and through the windows. There is a flood in our room. The water is up to our ankles. Talk about being out of code. If the city knew of this, these people would be fined or shut down. What's most shocking is that they actually charge us to live here. They collect 25% from our paychecks each week, yet the halfway house is considered a 'non-profit." Why on Earth are they charging us 25%? Even after the fact that most of us here are trying to rebuild. What's even more interesting is that they continue to collect that 25% from each of us when we no longer live here, when we have been sent to home confinement, to live with our families. They do so until we are completely done with the BOP, the Bureau of Prison. We have a specific date under the jurisdiction of the BOP and then the majority, who are under probation, begin a new process with their assigned probation officer. This can take months after we have been sent home, and they still continue to collect their money from us. This place is like a daycare. Not to mention, how is this even legal? God, I just hate being here.

I've been going to work with Judas for the last few days now. It's been incredibly surreal. He has been like an angel in my life. I met Judas not too long before I was indicted. We established a very strong professional friendship. His office is in South Beach and he specializes mostly in weight loss and smoking cessation. He is a solo practitioner, when we met I had a full practice with several practitioners in South Miami for over 14 years. He used to refer clients to us regularly.

Throughout my incarceration, Judas was like a brother. Honestly, he was better than my own blood-related brothers. He would write to me all the time. Judas sent me the entire collection of books by Dr. John Demartini for me to read. I remember how he used to Google all sorts of stuff that I was researching. He would print it and then mail it to me. There was a time I was researching some of humanity's worst atrocities, so he sent me a few pages on genocides. My friends at the camp thought I was crazy for reading those types of stories of people who were massacred. I was simply trying to understand why, as humans, we do what we do. He was incredibly supportive throughout the entire process.

During a visit at Coleman, Judas asked me what I was doing once I get out of prison? My reply was simple. I asked him, what am I supposed to do with a felony? My business had closed down and I had nothing left, nothing to my name. He replied that he knew what I was doing, he said I was going to join his practice and together we were going to do great things. I recall that moment like it was yesterday. Judas was a man of his word. He delivered. He has been here for me every step of the way. I will forever be grateful for his help no matter what lies before us. He is equally frustrated with the expectations that are placed upon me here at the halfway house. As I get to the office each day, I share with him all the stupidity that goes on. He wants to defend me and if possible report them but he's afraid that I will be reprimanded for it.

Each day I dress up like a doll in my old designer shoes and expensive handbags, only to take four buses to and from work. Public transportation in Miami is a nightmare. My clients have no idea that I'm living in a halfway house in the middle of the ghetto. They don't know that I just served nine months in a federal prison, and that I still have another seven months of home confinement with an ankle bracelet to go before I'm actually done with all this bullshit. They don't imagine anything, but, for me it's unsettling. I put on a costume to go to work and play a role. These clothes do not define me anymore. I'm acting, that's all this is. I'm having to forcefully step into the role that I have this all figured out when I really don't. Every morning, I try to tell myself that I am the person I used to be, the one who had it all under control, but, I'm not her anymore. So, I continue acting, smiling, and nodding along while I figure it out. I go to work to fix people's lives, resolve their issues, offer messages of empowerment and self-fulfillment when, unbeknownst to them, I just came from living inside a hellhole. At least I haven't lost my talent. I'm still amazing at my work. Not to brag, I think I'm actually better now than I was before. I guess having the shoe on the other foot certainly makes a difference. I got to play out many of my own client's roles while I was in prison. I got to suffer and endure tremendous hardship. It was my turn to get a taste of it and face my own demons.

On the bus, on my way to work, I notice the way I am looked at by the other passengers. They must think I'm ridiculous. Who is this woman? And why is she taking public transportation wearing a pair of Prada flats and a Louis Vuitton purse? The truth is, I had all this fancy crap from before I went to prison. I can't afford this right now. Even if I could, I would not purchase any of it. Believe me these brands do not define me. I am exactly like these people on the bus, we are equals, even if it doesn't seem that way. After a few days of being stared down, I've stopped wearing my fancy bags on the bus. I asked my mom to buy me a purse that didn't catch so much attention. I need to accept that I am no longer who I was. I don't care for any of that. I need to stop trying to resurrect her. Instead, I'm adjusting, and learning to take my challenges and convert them into strengths.

During most bus rides, I spend a lot of time thinking back to my divorce when I was 23 years old. I was a full-time college student with my ten-month old daughter, Amber, my four-year-old daughter, Gemeny, plenty of bills, and a part time income while starting my business. What methods worked for me then? I will use those again to get me through this. I'm putting a pair of blinders on just like I did then. I refuse to keep looking left and right. From now on, I will always be looking forward. There's no point in looking back. I owe it to the women in prison - my friends - to make something of myself again. I must persevere and overcome. This will not defeat me. I will adapt, like I always have. I am stronger, not weaker, for my experiences. I must remember this. I am in a process of becoming a new me. Ever evolving and honoring that. Rather than continue to romanticize the past, I will invest my energies here, in the now. I will focus on reintegrating into society as functional as I've always been.

At some point, when all of this is over, I would like to be involved, somehow, with prison reform; I want to tell the world what really goes on in our prison system. Perhaps, I can impact change in the minds of people about what really happens within the justice system. People need to know and understand the challenges that we face as ex-convicts. I don't care for victimhood, I will never be a victim of my circumstances. That is simply unacceptable to me. However, society needs to wake up, be compassionate and more aware. I want to be involved somehow in changing the laws. As felons, we lose our civil right to vote. There are currently 6.1 million Americans barred from voting because of felony disenfranchisement laws. Particularly, in Florida whose constitution permanently disenfranchises citizens with past felony convictions and grants only the governor the authority to restore voting rights. I want to be that voice, but fuck, it's so difficult. I want to do all this, but, there's this part of me that still feels so uncertain about who I am. I ask myself, who will believe me? Who the hell am I right now? I live in a damn halfway house for God's sakes.

Just yesterday, one of the women living at the halfway house was assaulted on her walk back from work just a few blocks from here. She too takes the bus, as do most of us. We are not allowed to carry any weapon for defense, even though we live in an incredibly dangerous side of town. Her bus dropped her off past 10 pm. When she arrives at the halfway house, clearly shaken and scared, she is being chastised for being late. Even after the fact that she explains to them what had just happened to her. I can't believe it. I went up to her and held her, but, was told I could not do so. It is against the rules. I felt so angry and so powerless. I wanted to kick the guy in the balls for being such an asshole, but, I keep my composure. I cannot believe this is happening even outside of prison. We are being disrespected, neglected, mistreated, dismissed, and they are getting away with it. We are just as valuable, just as important, as the rest. We have dreams, fears, and visions, just like everyone else. We need love just as badly, maybe even a little more. So then why are we so ostracized? When did we become the enemy?

It is so difficult to explain what these last few weeks have been like for me. During my first few days here, I was an outcast. Even worse, young adults babysit us. How condescending and embarrassing is it to be watched by undergrad students with no experience and who think they have some power over us because we are all convicts? They're in their early twenties completing the required hours to graduate. They don't understand us, and it doesn't feel like they care to. They simply enforce the outrageously outlandish and ridiculous house rules. They try to intimidate us by instilling fear that we can be sent back to prison at any time. Just today, I got here ten minutes late because I missed the bus coming back from work. I am so stressed out. I walk in and head to the cafeteria to eat and a few minutes after, I pass out in front of everyone while I'm in line getting my food. Thank God there is a guy right next to me as I am on my way down and he grabbed my head before it hit the concrete floor. They are calling fire rescue to make sure I'm ok. Turns out, it's all stress related. No, really?

The halfway house is a tease. You think you're free, but you're not. If I arrive even one minute late or early, I need to explain myself. The first few days, I went into explicit detail to account for my tardiness. Lately when asked why I am early, I snap, "because I got here early!" They look at me and roll their eyes. I'm pretty sure they equally dislike me. I'm tired of this treatment. They are all jerks here. The people who watch over us want to remind us that we're outcasts and that we are disempowered. Well, I'm taking my power back. I refuse to fail, even though we really are set up for failure. We're constantly reminded that our punishment isn't over and we could easily be thrown back into prison. This neighborhood is a nesting ground for drug use, drug trafficking, and violence. How are we expected to rise above this culture when we're shoved, face-first, into the same realities many are expected to overcome? I know I will not stumble in that respect - drugs are not my thing, they never have been, but many of the men and women in here with me struggle with that. They are addicts that were never taken to rehab or provided addiction programming. Instead, they were thrown in prison as a form of punishment and never learned to cope with their issues. They continued to numb their emotions with drugs. They're expected to live soberly from now on, but, they still don't know any better. This is all they have ever known. They need resources, support, counseling, not a curfew. This makes no sense. We are set up to fail and nobody gives a damn.

I'm trying to blend in a little bit better as each day passes. It doesn't happen right away, but it's happening. I'm no longer afraid to cross the street. I've accepted that reintegration is something we must deal with ourselves and in our own way. This has truly been a humbling experience. I look around and a voice tells me, "you're not going be doing this for the rest of your life." Then, I'll look at the faces of those beside me on the bus, the people who have been doing this for years, and I wonder how they do it. I have only admiration for their strength; their perseverance. I bow in gratitude. They are my greatest teachers. This is an interesting process, to say the least. I haven't struggled with my own identity so deeply like this in years. I don't know who I am anymore. All I know is that I am not who I used to be, I'm better. God damn it, I better be.

I know what is keeping me small. It's this persistent voice that continues to tell me I will fall again. That I'll find myself in the rat race again - the one I only escaped while I was in prison. A part of me wants to resist the flow of things because I'm terrified that I'll get sucked back into my old work habits. I keep checking in with myself, willing myself forward, too aware to fall into the old patterns. I don't want to work, work, work. I don't want to start doing again, at the expense of being. I am afraid, but, this desperation to become better is crucial. Right now, all I can focus on is getting my life back. Rising from these ashes is my priority. I want to be the successful woman I once was, but, without paying the price for it. I still need to figure that part out.

The thing is, before going to prison, I thought I had everything figured out. I was financially stable with a thriving hypnosis and coaching practice. I had a nice home, a plethora of friends, and, at one point, I was even engaged. For years, I was an avid traveler. I was convinced that I didn't lack anything. However, now that I'm back in the 'real world', I have nothing. I don't have a car. I have no home. No relationship. Nothing to claim as mine. I can't look at a single thing and say, 'this is mine." I'm raw, I'm naked, and yet in some strange way, it feels like I have everything I didn't have before. I feel free, self-aware, and purposeful. I do not want to exchange that for my old, so-called, successful life.

At some point, I came to the realization that I'm not so different from everyone else. We're creatures of habit, so of course we fall back into habits. I've slowly started to remember what I had forgotten. I forgot how much drive I've always had. I forgot how tenacious I am. I forgot everything I had ever learned - everything I'd been preaching for so long. I've had to remind myself of the days when I was 23 years old, divorced with two small daughters. I had no idea how I was going to make it, but I remained intentional. It's like I am twenty-three all over again. I am doing what worked for me in the past. I won't stop. It worked for me before, it will work again. The difference is, I can't just do, do and do. I must remember to let myself to just "be" during this process. To ride this like I'm riding a wave. I can't swim against the current or I will drown. I will remain focused on my goal: to lift myself from the ashes. I will never allow myself to fall victim. Little by little, as time unfolds and new challenges arise, I remind myself what prison taught me: everything is temporary. Both happiness and sadness are temporary. Anais Nin said, "Life is a process of becoming, a combination of states we have to go through. Where people fail is that they wish to elect a state and remain in it. This is a kind of death."

I elect the state that I am in. To this end, I forcefully elect to change my state. I know I need to be forceful and intentional because it is so easy to remain stuck. Yes, I am petrified. Yes, I am conflicted with doubt. Yes, yes. Of course. I am learning that fear is always with me. The concept of anyone eliminating fear altogether is a fallacy. It is part of the human experience. I elect to ride with fear, recognizing that it is always there and that is okay. I simply choose not to give it power. I am the driver, not fear. I understand that we compromise too easy when life becomes difficult. I must not follow my impulse to be weak.

I'm not doing this because I'm wiser or stronger than anyone else. On the contrary, I am broken right now. I feel like I just went to battle - I am deeply wounded. I am only capable of doing this because, at last, I am ready. Everything has led to this. It's finally time for me to use everything I have ever preached. My new mantra has become simple and powerfully true: So be it.

Chapter 2

July 11, 2012

Here we are. "Oh my God, Vamp. I don't want to go inside this fucking place. I can't do this. I simply can't. Please drive off. Let's run away together. Don't let me go inside. I can't do it. I just can't." I'm so afraid. What is going to happen to me?

He left me here. He is staring at me through the glass door, tears are running down his face and mine. The guard is processing me. She is nice, which feels strange. I thought it would be like in the movies. I was under the impression that she was going to be screaming at me already. What? She wants me to do what? Squat? No way. Get naked, cough and squat to my knees to see if I've hidden what? Inside what? Oh my God, this is so humiliating. How demoralizing is this? This woman is staring me blank in the face after she has watched me bend down and expose all of my private parts. Wait, I'm now in prison. I just showed her my pussy and ass. Let's leave the fancy words for when I get out. I'm here for a 21-month sentence but it feels like forever already. I'm probably going to be living with thugs and delinquents. People who have committed real crimes. I bet I'm the only one in this place that hasn't committed the crimes I was accused of. This is bullshit. Here I go. I'm handed these awful looking clothes; a hideous beige colored pair of boy looking pants with an equally hideous top. My new undies are suitable for any 80-year old grandma and my bras look like I'm ready to run a marathon. I guess I have to get used to this. This is my new life, for now.

I wonder what kind of women I will meet here. Are any of my co-defendants here? That would not be cool. They all probably knew what Griselda was doing. Who knows, maybe they too are innocent. Well, at least she won't be here. As part of the process, I'm being asked if I have anything against my co-defendants. Why are they asking me this? I don't even know most of them. I think they are done asking me questions. They called for an inmate to come get me. The inmate is walking me out of the office and into the compound where I have been sentenced to live for the next fourteen months. I'm quietly walking beside her while looking at my surroundings. There are a lot of buildings. I wonder what happens inside them. She is walking me to a building that faces a screened patio and the parking lot where I was just dropped off. Why aren't there any wired fences or gates surrounding this compound? Do people escape from prison often? I'm going to be living at F4. That's what the building is called. She walks me upstairs. My feet feel like they are dragging a ball and chain. I feel so heavy. As if I was being walked to a gas chamber. I just got to my new room. There are no bars. I thought I would live in a room with bars.

almost every weekend. In here, she is my family now. We get along very well, and it almost feels like she is the sister I never had. We are trying our best not to blame, but, it's so difficult. Inside these prison walls, you experience a roller coaster of emotions daily. Sylvia is very active, like me. We both walk outside on the track each day. It's our therapy time and a great reason to get out of our units. There isn't a moment of silence ever. The women never shut up. They drive us crazy.

I've made a few other friends. I probably should be careful, they say you can't trust people in prison. You have to watch your back all the time. I don't know, maybe it's that wolf verses sheep thing I heard before coming here. Clearly, I'd rather be the wolf than a sheep, that's for sure. I mean, wolves eat the sheep right? I don't want to get eaten. I keep conversations with people as short and simple as possible. More 'hi', and 'bye' than anything else. But, there are a few women I've befriended.

My bunkee, Lisa is really nice. I've gotten to know her a lot better. She doesn't talk much, and she is always either reading the bible, or listening to the news on her radio. She goes to work really early each morning. She's been sharing some of her childhood stories with me. She's had a really tough life. If you ask me, I really don't think she should be here. Her ex-boyfriend was convicted of meth distribution and she was charged with co-

conspiracy. We both come from very different backgrounds. Mine isn't any better than hers, it's just different. I have a feeling God knew what he was doing when he placed me inside the same room with Lisa. Before I came to Coleman, I thought I had heard it all: the wildest, weirdest, and toughest stories anyone has heard. However, none were remotely as strange and heart-wrenching as what I'd heard here thus far. These stories only make some days seem like years. Everything just feels so long and unfulfilled. It is difficult to be inside the unit. Imagine being inside a space the size of a warehouse, surrounded by obnoxious women screaming at each other, laughing loudly, and eating messily all the time. If I try escaping to the microwave room, I'll find it just as packed and noisy as the rest of the unit. Some women prepare their meals at 4:00 am! Looking for solace, I'll head outside to walk the track with Sylvia any chance we get. We can both walk and look up at the sky unlike the prison, the sky was boundless. We can gaze at the clouds and try to keep our sanity as much as we can. There isn't much to look forward to at this point of our lives. I exercise regularly; knowing that doing so is good for my mind as well as my body. I read books and I've vowed to meditate everyday. I always ask the same question in desperation: God why am I here? Show me please! These words ring in my ears, day after day after day. I even got into the habit of asking God for answers through the books I read. Many times, I'll put my right hand

31

worse; doing things they are not supposed to, such as crawl into the beds of other inmates they are having relationships with for sex. Can you blame them? Some of them have been here for so many years. They all need love. It's human nature to seek love.

Falling asleep is a challenge. Staying asleep is another ordeal. If it isn't my other bunkmate loudly opening a locker at 3:00 am looking for food, it's one of the guards doing count time at odd hours of the night. They walk with their flashlights on, pointing it right at our faces while we sleep and dangle their keys. It is literally impossible to sleep through the night.

There simply is no consideration for us. Some guards are so rude, they'll be laughing and making jokes while counting at 3 am. I've had maybe, one full night of sleep since I got here. It's normal to wake up three to four times a night. How could we not, with the uncomfortable, stiff mattresses we are expected to sleep on? The old stinky mattress sinks in and causes immense pain in my back and neck. I can feel the metal wires inside my mattress pinching my back sometimes. I wake up sore all over my body. Some mornings I feel like a truck has run over me. Every tiny little muscle and bone hurts. My neck is always stiff and I get several recurring headaches a week. I'm not expecting daily life in prison to be a walk in the park, by any means, even if it is a camp. Yet, I don't understand why institutions such as these were built to punish instead of rehabilitate. There's simply no need to have anyone of us living in these conditions. What's horrifying is that for some of the women in here, this place is heaven in comparison to where they were before being incarcerated. Some even say that being here is the best thing that has happened to them. I can only imagine what their lives have been like for them to say such a thing. I need to go off to meditate and find some peace or else, I'm just going to go crazy.

Whenever I meditate, I am desperate to feel purpose, guidance, and clarity of some sort. I ask for a sign from above. At times, I give up on this search. I'll drop my head and force myself to trust that God or some higher power is listening, and His response is silent. The answers will come at the perfect time, I'll tell myself. Then I remember: I am not a patient woman. I am a control freak. I want answers right now. I pray on. Feeling as empty as my stomach feels most days. I walk off to meet a friend.

Alice, one of the women at the prison, is here because of conspiracy for tax evasion. Alice and her husband claim they are innocent, but when they attempted to defend themselves from the tax evasion charge, a judge sentenced them to 48 months in prison. Some argue that the Internal Revenue Service is not an agency of the United States but rather a private corporation, because it

On occasion, as I walk on the track, I watch the other women and wonder: what are they thinking about? I've learned to admire many of them. Particularly those who have small children and are serving long sentences. Somehow, I've never quite known compassion the way I am experiencing it now. It's like I'm experiencing all their pain in my own flesh. I sit and remember many of my sessions at the office where I had listened to painful, traumatizing events being shared by my clients. The type of stories you think only happens in movies. Even still, in all my years of private practice, I have never felt this way. I am humbled by these women. I've experienced a shift: a desire to listen and internalize what they are feeling. I had been so understanding and empathetic in my career, but this is something different. It's hard to describe with words. It's as if there is this oneness in our pain. Here I am feeling the same pain, the stifling hole in my chest that they feel. I watch them in awe.

One of the first things I am learning while I'm here is that whoever we were before we entered the doors of this camp no longer matter. Some of us are doctors, dentists, mortgage brokers, nurses, drug users and dealers, but in the end, we are all the same; a number located on a red ID tag we are forced to carry at all times. Not even my worst enemy should ever feel what we are feeling. That was just it, we are feeling this way together. Collectively, we share these emotions behind all of the impersonal greetings and head nods. We feel each other's pain and desperation. We are all in this torment together. Neither race nor culture or even convictions separates any of us. For the first time, we are all one and the same.

I met Teresa today. She is serving a 22-year sentence because she chose to go to trial instead of accepting the plea deal being offered to her by her prosecutor. If Teresa had taken the plea, she would have served an 18-month sentence. Teresa had three children at the time she was sentenced. She was a single mother and she's an absolutely admirable woman. She teaches yoga and art classes to the inmates. She's already served 13 years of her sentence. I look to her to feel a sense of hope. She is beautiful, inside and out. She reflects a sense of peace and acceptance unlike anyone else here. Teresa worked in finance for a very large corporation that was part of a huge fraud scandal. She was indicted for conspiracy. She was an employee there and they claimed she knew what the company was doing. Everyone that was indicted was sentenced, including the companies' attorneys. Teresa was innocent. She couldn't say if the company she worked for was guilty or not because, she simply didn't know how the company earned their money. She just worked there.

With most federal defense attorneys, her attorney lied assuring she had a very good chance of winning if they went to trial. After he took the very last bit of her savings, she agreed to go to trial. The judge sentenced her to twenty years in federal prison, mentioning that she wasted his time by not accepting the plea bargain. Should she had taken it, it would have only been an 18-month sentence. She was taken immediately into custody and wasn't allowed to even say goodbye to her children and family.

Like her, there are so many more. It seems that whenever I sit down somewhere, I'm approached by someone with another unfortunate story. At times, I look around and think of how many women are here serving time for either something they didn't do or serving an unjust sentence for something they did. I mean, let's get something straight, none of these women are here for violent offenses. As a matter of fact, only 18% of the people in prisons are serving time for nonviolent offenses in the State of Florida. These women are all either white collar crimes or drug charges. Nearly one out of four have children back home, and families who depend on them financially. This is ridiculous. in America, 1 in 100 adults is currently locked up. Something is wrong here. These numbers are mind-boggling. I'm getting nauseous thinking about all of this. Come to think of it, I feel nauseous a lot since I arrived just a few weeks ago. I'm not pregnant, but, there are a few women here who are. Being pregnant in prison is one of the worst things I can think of. The new mothers are stripped from their newborns a day or two after they give birth. The babies are either taken to foster care or given to an appointed custodial parent.

There are days I feel sick to my stomach from the stories I hear and from the research I do to learn more about how the prison system works. There is one lady in her late fifties who shared her story with me during lunch. She was a pharmacist charged with conspiracy. It didn't surprise me; most of us are here because of drugs or conspiracy charges. This lady is serving a six-year sentence. She went to trial, was found innocent by the jury, but the judge overruled the verdict and found her guilty. The irony is that she was being charged for a crime that her ex-husband committed. If that's not insane, I don't know what is! She got pinned with the crime instead. What the hell is that?

This story has stayed with me. I'm appalled and convinced of the injustices going on in our country. The more I think about all this, the more the anger rises from my stomach and overwhelms my head with anger and total disgust. These women have no idea the impact they are having on me. I always rush to my unit and write down their stories, so I won't forget. Some days, I listen to multiple stories from different women in the compound. Sometimes I wonder if these stories are good for me to hear. I always feel worse after I walk away to document what they've shared. I feel the anger down in the very pit of my stomach. It's a feeling of helplessness and hopelessness that rises. An almost uncontrollable urge to punch a wall. The sentences are too unfair. Even for those who committed their crimes. There are people serving life sentences for selling three ounces of meth for God's sakes. What is that? How can sentences like these exist in America of all places? I go on to replay their stories in my head over and over until I finally fall asleep in my bunk.

Today is another day. I feel a burst of energy and I brought myself to the track to go for a walk. It just rained, and the sky is still gray. The outskirts of the camp are damp. I walk around the track with my friend Vicky and Sylvia with so much force. I still think I don't fit in, though the reality is that I am like everyone else here. Most of the women in the camp are like me: hardworking mothers, wives, daughters and sisters of people back in the real world. They are like other woman I've met before. After a few times around the track, I go sit on a wet chair near a tree with a strange feeling of emptiness that had just come over me. I looked at the large oak tree and remembered the tree in the movie Avatar. I wondered what it would be like if that tree could hear me. Suddenly, I go back to the unit to shower and head over to the library. The library has become my favorite spot. My own little oasis, in this wretched place, where I can write without the fear that I'd get caught by the guards documenting all the horrific crap I am witnessing here. For instance, inmates are the ones to teach the GED class to the other inmates, but, when inspection time comes around, the staff warns the class they cannot mention a word about this to any of the inspectors. Inspections happen every couple of months. A group of inspectors travel from Washington to visit the camp. They come to confirm the rules are being followed and that the inmates are receiving what we are required according to the policies. On the day of the inspection we are served a pretty decent meal, plus, they have a few inmates pressure clean the walls of the camp, providing us with Clorox to clean the bathrooms, and all sorts of other forbidden cleaning products we aren't allowed to have in prison. What the hell? Aren't they breaking the law? These people are unbelievable.

Everything has become so autonomous, just like in real life. I wake up around 5:00 am and later eat a piece of muffin for breakfast (if we can call it a muffin), hit the track for a good two hours, then shower. By then, it's time for recall, so, I'll head back inside the unit and get ready for count. Then it's back out to lunch around 10:30 am. Soon after, I walk to the library or under the famous tree and read, write, and just look around for another few hours. Maybe take an art or yoga class, then back at 3:30 pm for recall again. By this time, it is already dinner at 4:30 pm. Afterwards, we can go to the track or take another class, and then finally recall again at 8:30 pm. At this point, we can't be out of our units until the next day. Either I watch some TV or lay in bed after checking my emails. This is the routine day-in and day-out. I didn't come here to work for the feds but I'm so bored that I think it's time for me to get a job.

Some of the jobs available to us are driving a forklift, landscaping, or driving a lawn mower in the hot searing sun. Some women work at Unicor inside a boiling hot warehouse counting parts or putting together desks that are then used at government offices throughout the country. My bunkee Lisa works at Unicor. Others work as mechanics fixing automobiles. I signed up to work as an orderly, which means I get to mop and clean the recreational room. Who would have thought? I'm very excited about my 6¢ an hour job. The highest paid job is at Unicor, where you run the risk of cutting a finger or injuring your back. You get paid a whopping 43¢ an hour, merely $60 a month or so. It's a form of slavery, a capitalist horror show. Apparently, that sort of stuff is still happening in the US, but only inside our prison system. Similar to many undocumented immigrants that arrive in the US who also work for less than the minimum wage. This treatment of 'others' is incredibly unfair and excruciating to see in person. One can read about it, but, there is a major difference to live it, and living it makes you feel powerless. I'm not against working, as it does offer the opportunity for some who have no work experience, a chance to learn a new skill, what I am against, is the pay. Slavery was abolished in the 13th amendment in 1865. Therefore, we shouldn't

48

be forced to work and receive this exiguous form of payment. Perhaps, that is why prison population has risen eight times more since 1970. It's like a cesspool of inhumane and unconstitutional acts that are being committed right under our noses. It's a fact that needs to be spoken about.

Regardless of the meager pay, we are expected to buy everything for ourselves in commissary. We have to purchase soap, shampoo, conditioner, hand cream, snacks, stamps, and so forth. One would think these items were inexpensive, whereas they are anything but cheap! Prices are marked up at a higher price than in stores. It did not take long for me to learn that prison was a business. No wonder why most people here are serving time unjustly. Now, I understand why my attorney told me that the federal government wins 95% of its cases. I researched that, since Coleman is a privately owned prison, the owners of this compound receive an estimated $32k annually for each inmate. In comparison to New York or California which is the most expensive, with an average cost of $60,000-$75,000 per prison inmate. This is why nine out of ten people involved in a federal crime are sent to prison. It makes perfect sense to keep us in camp instead of giving us probation or house arrest. We are all basically considered guilty from the beginning of an investigation, which is why we are all practically forced to plead guilty even though many of us, myself included, wanted to go to trial to defend

spending an additional 17 years in prison makes me want to vomit.

What kind of system is this? How can someone who is an addict, God knows what kind of childhood traumas, be condemned to such an obscene amount of time for selling and using meth? Why haven't they placed her in a rehab center instead? Why haven't they given her the opportunity to detox and address the issues that brought the addiction in the first place? Why not place addicts in a program that is suitable to help and prepare them to go out into society with a stronger self-esteem and a desire to live a better life? Instead, they are brought here to prison where their issues are never addressed. They are not detoxed or treated with therapy and rehabilitation. They are sentenced for decades, thrown back into society to fend for themselves. They are left with a felony conviction, with no education, or any help, and most of the time, no one waiting for them to offer support. How can she be expected to make it in the outside world? Many states with a felony conviction make it nearly impossible for someone to succeed. There are states where public assistance and public housing are banned to felons. Felonies, oftentimes, will cut you off from the possibility of getting certain jobs. We have all seen those applications asking "have you ever been convicted of a crime?" This question alone makes an interview impossible. You haven't even met your potential boss yet, but, you are already being asked and possibly judged for a crime that was committed, God knows how long ago. What is the point of serving time for your crime if even after you have fulfilled your sentence, you still have to face the same adversities that probably brought you to prison in the first place? Literally, disqualifying you from any potential of starting a new life. How can something of this level of importance be so inconsequential in this country?

75% of these women lost their families when they were sentenced; even their children were taken from them and placed in foster homes. That 32-year-old woman didn't even know where her child was placed because the government takes away all your rights. I cannot imagine what my life would be without my daughters or not knowing their whereabouts. I cannot imagine how this woman must be feeling inside. The only way I can explain this complete disregard for human life is money. She is a profit to this institution. I get it, they want her to fail again so she ends up back here in prison. This is how they make their money. It's like a money machine that never stops producing. It never ends. The cycle never stops. Ok, she committed the crime, no doubt, but a 22-year sentence? Are you kidding me? Who did she kill? Or rape? I am so angry towards humanity. Yet, you see all these politicians constantly breaking the law. They are exempt. They are untouchable. All these lobbyist receiving funds to support campaigns for corrupt politicians whom pass policies that only benefit their pockets. It's all so backwards. 600,000 are released from prison every year. Yet, why do two-thirds of those inmates end up back in prison, some without having even committed a crime? Because somehow, they violated their parole or probation. That means, something as simple as missing your appointment with your probation officer or not being able to make it on time when they call you while at work to leave and go pee to see if you have used any drugs. That is just crazy. It's due to all the challenges they face once they are released. For most of them, anyway, satisfying these conditions is literally impossible. They make it as such so you're set up to fail.

After shaking these thoughts aside, I decide to go outside to meet with Vicky. My crazy-Cuban friend. Poor Vicky has already been to prison once before. She's here now for a totally different charge. One that was unfolding while she was just finishing up with her probation from her first case. Vicky is loud and has a great sense of humor. I appreciate her for that. We don't get to laugh as often as we'd like, but, she makes Sylvia and I laugh a lot with the outlandish things that come out of her mouth. She says that she is committed to losing weight during her 18-month sentence. I meet up with her at the track and at the gym for Zumba classes every day. She lives in the unit underneath ours. She isn't allowed to come to our unit, but, Vicky doesn't always follow the rules. To no surprise, she shows up at our unit often and unexpectedly. If it weren't for these moments, what would be of us? My favorite day is Friday. Every Friday, Teresa, Daisy, Sylvia and I go outside near the old banyan tree and we have happy hour. Each of us brings something to eat. I'm in charge of the Sangria. I mix three cans of Sprite with three equal parts of water and four small Hawaiian Punch flavored bags inside a large water jar. If I'm able to steal an apple or orange from Mainline, I cut it up into little pieces and add it to the Sangria. I've become the official bartender of our group. The truth is my friends won't let me prepare anything to eat fearing it won't taste good. They are well aware I suck in the kitchen. We sit together, and Daisy recites poems she has written about each of us. We laugh a lot and make these moments memorable.

Today I met a new inmate. She arrived two days earlier. She was a chiropractor who'd been sentenced to five years in prison because of some seminar tickets she had sold years earlier. Apparently, the company selling the tickets was indicted and along with the indictment, she was charged for conspiracy for selling said tickets. At the time she was indicted, she was living in Costa Rica. She is an American woman who was forced to serve two years of her sentence in Costa Rica until all the paperwork had been completed and sent back to the US for extradition. After listening to her story, I started feeling a bit stressed. I don't know if she was involved in the fraudulent ticket sales or not, all I know is that a five-year sentence is a long time for something like this. These judges throw these outlandish sentences as if they were throwing Reese's Pieces candy to the audience. I'd like to see some of them serve a month in prison. They should see what it's like to be here. Most wouldn't make it past a month. Who came up with these sentencing guidelines? They are unfair. The system is broken. This isn't the way to correct society. I'm hitting the showers, checking my emails, will wait for the mail, and lay in bed until count at 10:00 pm. I think I've had enough for today. I can probably get a law degree with all that I have learned about our prison system. I just can't believe this wasn't a topic I ever cared for. I feel so ignorant.

Waking up the next morning and regretting I did not die in my sleep. I feel this way often. Not because I'm suicidal, but, there are days that the feeling is so heavy, especially after listening to so many stories from the other inmates, I just want to close my eyes and never wake up. It's shocking that these thoughts even cross my mind but I'm so sick and tired of this place. I'm so fed up with the fact that I have been caught in this fishnet of sorts. Within a system in my own country that is intentionally broken to benefit other people's pockets at the expense of families being divided. People's lives completely ruined. It's a realization that burns a hole in my heart because I happen to be on the inside of it. I could almost hear Leon, whispering to me: 'this is all an illusion. Remember the technology, it's all an illusion, none of it is real.' I consider him a brother, a best friend. We met a few years ago. Leon is charming and has a way of making women fall for him easily. I, on the other hand, never fell for that trick. I did find him attractive, once, back when we first met, but, my connection with him is at a deeper level that is non-romantic. We never even thought about being intimate. We are still very good friends. We used to get into deep conversations about life and spirituality. He is convinced we were all living inside a Matrix, like the movie, where the film touches the core of our beings as sentient lifeform. Thoughtful beings able to ponder their own existence. Leon always says he believes in me. He thinks I could change the way the world viewed itself. At times, I thought I could too, until my sentencing came around. On that day, I began to question everything. Perhaps, so do most people in a similar situation. I mostly question God and His role in all this.

It's funny how people find God in prison. I used to joke about it before coming to prison. I'd say, God either lives in church, hospitals or in prison. Now I'm convinced. 70% of the women here claim they have found God. They go to the chapel and read the Bible all day long. They preach the word of Christ or Jehovah or whatever they call Him. I think it's quite interesting to see this redemptive attitude in all of them. I ponder on how this takes place. Could it be that when we hit bottom, it is innate for all human beings to gravitate to a force that is bigger, stronger or more magnificent than we are? Did all these women seek God because collectively it was what almost everyone else is doing? So many women, and most of them preaching salvation of some sort. Yet, I'm here constantly questioning His existence. It's all perceptual I assume. Perception itself is relative. How we perceive things determines the meaning and thereby influences our experiences. Perception is a construct of our experiences, our environment, our beliefs, and our society. At the end of the day, it is not absolute. It is not real; it is simply how we perceive things. It's relative because it's different for every individual. This is completely contingent on the lens through which we are looking at the world. The lens we look through creates our perception.

Chapter 3

There's Linda, the little Vietnamese lady who is missing almost every one of her teeth. Linda walks around smiling all day long. She is as sweet and genuine as one can be. She speaks broken English. She is always near the tree feeding the cats. I met Linda at the chapel once when I was trying to sign up to the meditation classes. I had gone in there to attend a Buddhist class that was being offered by an outside group that visits prisons. When I arrived, it was the little Vietnamese lady, and me. No one came to teach the class, so she sat next to me. I remember feeling kind of lost that day. We then engaged in conversation. To no surprise, Linda is also here for conspiracy as well. Apparently, her late husband was the one being charged, but, since he was not around any longer, they charged her for it. Whether her husband committed the crime or not, he was dead and could not defend himself, or confirm that she was involved. They gave Linda a one-year sentence for conspiracy since she was married to him. Poor lady, she still doesn't know what either of them had done wrong. Linda said to me, 'God will give you lots of money and happiness when you get out. He will give you a lot of it,'. She smiles, we say goodbye and off she goes to feed the cats.

The funny thing is, not all of the money or fame will ever make up for my time in Coleman. At

to anything or anyone? Either way, I feel impotent. In the past, I would have stepped in and resolved the problem. This Wonder Woman does not feel wonderful right now. I want to transcend the situation by trying to look at it from another angle, yet the emotions continue to get in my way. My ego keeps pushing through with all it's might. After all, it is easier to blame her dad then to allow Gemeny to learn from this situation and endure it as it is intended for her. I have to be honest though, this is on her more than it is on him. I guess I miss her so much. I know all of this is part of her lesson. I just can't wait to see her.

I miss my family so much. I haven't seen them for so long. Today they are visiting. I am so anxious today and everyone is noticing. The thought of seeing my family again gives me goosebumps. I have been counting the hours until morning, tossing and turning all night long. With each glance at my watch, the hours seem longer. Full of stress and anticipation, I get up at 5:00 am and begin getting ready. I keep glancing out my window, which faces the parking lot. It is still very dark, but, I see a car come in, I could tell they are lost, not sure if they have found what they are looking for. The car stops frequently as it circles around the parking lot. It's my dad. He is here with my family two hours early! Most Cubans are late to everything, but, not my dad. It was so like him to always arrive earlier than expected. He doesn't believe in ever being late, especially now that he was visiting his daughter in prison. They must have left Miami at midnight. Since everyone was sleeping I could not run out of my unit and let them know that I saw them. I'm here! I love you, please save me.

This was my day to be with those I loved so much! After much reflection in here, I realize that most of the time, I took those moments for granted. You never expect that you will be ripped from your loved ones until it happens. I've been waltzing around the unit staring at my watch. Time is going by so slowly but it's almost time for us to walk to the visiting room. Finally, I'm going outside with Sylvia and Vicky who are also waiting for visitors. As we all gather, waiting for our names to be called, I feel a sudden tightness in my stomach. I look up and my daughter, Gemeny, is waving to me with a big smile. I desperately want to run to her arms, but, I know I can't. My eyes are watery. I see my youngest daughter, Amber, as they are patting her down, searching for anything that was considered contraband. Once inside, I rush to them and hold them tightly. Tears begin to stream down my cheeks as I clung to them. There is all this love surrounding us, it feels as if no one else inside the visiting room even existed. It is just the five of us. My parents look old, emotionally worn, but I try not to focus on this. They are trying to look happy for me, but, I know how they really feel and the hell they are going through.

We all sit at a rickety table, though it isn't long before this overwhelming, I-want-to-run-and-throw-up feeling takes over. There is so much to tell them, but only so little time. Besides us, there are 10 to 15 other families just as excited and rambunctious. It is loud and crowded; the tables nearly touch each other. It reminds me of being inside a concert but with no music playing, everyone trying to speak over one another.

I try to refocus and play referee between the girls who are fighting with each other to get my attention. My kids are dumbfounded by the military outfits we have to wear during visitation. They express how manly I look, even though I have makeup on, and some cheap perfume I borrowed from Sylvia that she bought from commissary. As the hours pass, I keep glancing at the clock on the wall, knowing that by 3:00 pm, our moment will be over. Again, the anxiety of them leaving steals my thoughts. The revolting feeling is taking over once again. I am grieving their absence and they haven't even left yet! My mom insists that I eat. She seems convinced that we are not fed properly in prison, no kidding. Meanwhile, the only things available inside the visiting room are vending machines filled with junk food. All of it looks so good. I keep wishing my stomach had a reserve tank, so I could save some for later. We play several games of Uno. I have to admit, it is a lot of fun. I take them outside to the patio area, so they could see the rest of the compound. Unfortunately, I can't take them anywhere else, but they have an opportunity to see some of it. All that mattered was that we are together again, even if only for a little while.

It's time to say goodbye, all I want to do is hold on and never let go. I want to run to their car and jolt out of the camp. Tears run down our faces once more. We hug, and I whisper in my daughter's ears. I love you. Don't ever forget all that I have taught you. Love, forgive, and don't keep any anger in your heart. This is all happening because I chose it before I was born.

I walk looking at their faces as they exit the room. I am now in line with one of the guards and the rest of the inmates just said their farewells to their loved ones, as well. I am placed in a room with two other women and the guard. Today they are strip searching us before we can exit the visiting room and return to our units. I stare at the two other women in the face. One is an older lady. She looks mortified. They are asking all of us to strip naked in front of each other. I begin to take off all my clothes, one piece of garment at a time. I'm trying not to look at the other women in fear that they will feel shame. I honestly, don't even care anymore if I'm asked to strip naked. It gets to a point that you begin to feel sorry for the guard who has to stand there watching us bend over and show her our ass holes than anything else. The old lady is crying. I feel sorry for her. This is so unnecessary. I know many inmates do bring back contraband from their visits, but, the guard could have had one inmate strip at a time. Is this even allowed? Probably not, but who the hell will say anything. It's always their word against ours. The guard quickly tells us to get dressed and hands us back our red ID cards. I exit the doors without looking back. The rest of the day, my body aches as if I had been in a boxing match. I keep feeling nauseous and sick to my stomach. I constantly hold my tears in because I am afraid that if I cry, I won't stop. Heartbroken at the fact that I don't know when I will see my family again, I try to distract myself by watching a movie in the TV room until count time before dinner.

As I sit here trying to stay focused on the TV, I realize that we all have difficulty being present in the moment. Somehow, we're always drawn to something in our past we did or something we never got to do. Yet, I know that both past and future only exists in our minds. The only real moment was the present. I slowly bring myself back to this moment. I watch the movie playing and stop making illogical comparisons. It is as I had feared, spending time with my family was the best and worst thing that has happened to me since my arrival at Coleman. Seeing their faces for the first time since I self-surrendered, I was back to ground zero. All the meditations, all the visualizations, self-talk, and progress I had achieved, could not get me out of the rut-like state of mind I was now in. I am overwhelmed by feelings of doom, anger and bitterness. Like the Gladiator movie I was watching, I too wanted to hurt someone for all of my suffering. I wanted to cry and run back into the arms of my family. So, off I go to the showers and, shortly after, struggle to sleep and wish I didn't wake up to endure another day in this hell I've been summoned to live in.

Once a week, we are required to participate in a class called, Getting It Right. I don't quite understand why I need to take this stupid class, because the booklet only talks about relapse and our so called 'criminal minds', by which I'm very offended. I do not have a criminal mind. As a matter of fact, many of the women here do not adhere to said thoughts. This is all bullshit, but, I know doing so keeps me busy and not pontificating why I am here. The room is filled with about 15 to 20 women who all live in different units. Sylvia and Vicky are taking this stupid class with me because it is expected that we take it to be considered 'rehabilitated.' What a crock of shit! While waiting for everyone to settle in, Lindsay begins speaking and introducing herself. She was an attorney in the 'real world' as we like to call it. She's already served seven of her 10-year sentence. She shares that she used drugs and alcohol, especially meth. Lindsay's only son died at nine years old and her mom died shortly after that. She was here for a drug charge because her ex was caught with drugs and had pointed the finger at her. Now this caught my attention, I was listening attentively. Here is this woman who lost her nine-year-old son, charged for a crime where her involvement was that of a user, not a seller, and is now instructing this particularly depressing class. For a moment, I'm imagining her pain and desperation, which led her to use drugs to alleviate what she must have been going through at the time. You can tell she had aged immensely, probably due to the many drugs she used.

Clearly, she is an educated woman who underwent a very difficult experience and didn't know how to cope. Could you blame her? Compassion kicked in as my heart and chest felt a tight squeeze. The room suddenly became a few degrees colder. I feel like I am inside an ice box as I sit here staring at her while she is sharing her story. She expresses how scared she feels to be outside in the world once she is released. She has no family, no resources, she has nothing left and has lost everything including herself. Unfortunately, she can't go and practice law again. She has been disbarred because of her crime. Do we blame the system? Do we blame the drug use? Do we blame her boyfriend? Do we blame her? Can we honestly say that she deserves what she got? All I know, is that she wasn't getting the tools she needed in here to address the underlying cause of her problems. Prison isn't the solution. It isn't hard to see how truly ineffective it is to place an addict in prison. How could this help her, other than the obvious? If she doesn't have the drugs, then she can't use them, but, how does this help her to overcome and understand the root of her problems? How can being in prison offer her healing and an opportunity to repair what broke her in the first place? I was so angry and felt so impotent listening to her story and not being able to offer her a solution. After all, I have heard hundreds of stories similar to hers because of my profession. But in here, it felt different. I was kicked off my high horse and am now at face level with everyone. I'm aware that we must be willing to give up our story, which is nothing more than our personal history. We must not define ourselves through our stories, but, learn from it instead. Clearly, I know at a higher level the outcomes we experience are ultimately neither good or bad. Simply put, they are the results of something we created at some point in our minds. I desperately try to remind myself that our darkest sorrows have an equal amount of joy, even if at times we cannot see or understand it. Perhaps, it's impossible to see it if we are coming from the same mindset that created it. So, what if, instead, we decided that everything that happens to us is an opportunity? I wonder how being in here could be an opportunity for these women who obviously needed the help. How could they benefit from this, at all, if once they are released they are forced to face a society that will reject them? How can being in a fermenting situation be opportunistic?

Desperately I try to remember all the wisdom Elizabeth has shared with me throughout the years during my kabbalah classes. I search for something that would help me understand without letting my ego get in the way again to judge. Leon calls Elizabeth 'The Oracle.' She is one of the wisest women I've ever met. A person genuinely filled with unconditional love and an enormous amount of compassion. I have been seeing Elizabeth for over 14 years now. I used to take all of her classes on spirituality. Elizabeth would say, 'we are never given a problem we can't handle or solve.' That's where I concluded that maximum growth only occurs in the very heart of chaos. She always preaches about how all of our problems help us grow. I agree that I need to rise above my problems, so the solutions become more visible. I have to convince myself not to allow these circumstances or the stories I hear derail me. Deep down inside the core of my soul I know I will rise above all of this as a much better person.

I'm not going to allow my experiences here destroy me anymore than they have. This is a personal promise. I want to come from a place of love; a place where I can forgive myself for having co-created these experiences. A place where I can also forgive this system for being part of the reason why we are all here. I have to believe that I will accomplish this, somehow. Shit, I still have so many more months to go before I get out. I want to stay optimistic, but, it all seems so dark from in here. Yet, the clearer I become with my purpose and intention, the more aligned I will be with infinite wisdom. I understand that the meaning of life differs from person to person and situation to situation. It is necessary for me to reach a point of acceptance that goes beyond any intellectual reasoning.

In my mind, I search underneath my thoughts and my ego, in hopes of finding an inherent order that will allow me to better understand all of this. Learning to be centered, I know I will find the power to overcome just about anything; to willingly experience that every moment is an opportunity. But how may one embrace such a thing if everyone was living inside their own kind of hell in here? I'm not referring to a hell as in a place you go to. I'm talking about a state of mind you live in. We all live in some form of hell inside these prison walls. For some people, it's the fact that they were caught committing their crimes and they are no longer free. Other people's hell is the reality that they cannot be there to raise their children and be the type of parental role models they could be. Some women in here, experience hell by constantly acting from a place of anger and hate. Maybe through meditation they too could find their peace. Meditation is the key, especially for me, who is always trying to control everything. I need to meditate more. I need to digest these stories differently before they consume me. Some days I feel consumed by them. It's so crazy though, to think I've been in a career where all I've heard are traumatic stories for the past 14 years and I was never once affected by any of it until now. It doesn't make sense to me. Why are these women's stories affecting me so much? Why is it that their stories are plunging a dagger into my heart?

I must meditate. It helps me to think that everything will fall into some kind of order someday. Meditation helps me tap into those parts of me that I can learn to accept without conditions. I frequently head outside to meditate for about 20 minutes after breakfast. I am in search of peace, and, hope that my questions will be answered somehow. At times feeling betrayed and abandoned by the universe, I have felt a sense of paralysis has taken over my faith. As much as I try to convince myself that God is a cynic who plays chess with us, I know that it is my ego that wants me to believe this. Deep down I feel an inherent connection to an energy I cannot explain, but, one which I believe totally exists. God isn't a He or a She in my perception. God is an energy, the universe. I am a part of this universe. I must rise above my ego and remember what I have always known. All our experiences are purposeful especially the most brutally painful ones.

For the first time since I arrived, there is a feeling of calm inside me today. So, I'm challenging myself to strip away my ego as best as I could. The ego leads us in believing that we are all victims of our circumstances. However, I've always believed that there aren't any victims or villains in any situation. As Neale Donald Walsch once said, "We are all volunteers." Doesn't that sound crazy?

74

The idea that we actually volunteer for an experience only makes sense when we define that particular experience as something pleasant. The moment we define it as unpleasant, we refuse to believe that we volunteered to experience it. The fact is, we did. We all volunteer to play a role in all of our experiences. I know that most religions don't agree with this. Hence, I've never followed any religion. I'm more of a spirituality kind of gal.

As a child, I grew up without any affiliation to religion. At the age of ten, I remember being forced to do communion at a nearby Catholic Church when we lived in South Beach. I never understood why my mom expected me to receive communion. We weren't catholic. Quite frankly, we only went to church to attend a wedding or a mass after the passing of someone we knew. Nevertheless, I took those classes and remember thinking what was being preached made no sense to me at all. It felt empty, vague and somewhat dishonest. In lieu of my rebellion, I began to search for something else. Something didn't make sense to me behind that whole 'Catholic Guilt' thing. I didn't agree with anything I was being told at church. A part of me refused it. I wanted answers that made sense to me.

At about 11 years old, I had already read several books on metaphysics, hypnosis and paranormal topics that included extraterrestrial visits from other planets. I was that funny looking cuckoo kid you see in some movies that talked to herself, but, luckily wasn't schizophrenic. Most kids were climbing trees or riding bikes around my neighborhood, not me. I never actually learned to ride a bike. 25 years later, I still don't know how to ride a damn bike, but I never did consider myself to be a deprived child. I guess I will add that on my bucket list when I leave prison. I have to learn to ride a bike at some point!

I grew up in a lower-middle class household. We arrived in the US in the 80s during the Cuban Mariel Boatlift when I was only four years old. That's right, I came here on a Banana Boat, as many call it. This was when Castro allowed a few thousand people to leave the country of Cuba, in exile. Off we went to the land of the free. My parents were hard workers; as a child, they tried to be good providers. I don't remember needing anything. Sure, we had financial struggles, like any immigrant. I never expected anything, I also didn't ask for more than was given to me. On the contrary, at the age of 11, I was contracted to work on a few episodes of a television series for a bilingual program called Saludos. It was something that resembled Sesame Street, where I'd talk to this puppet that worked at a store. It never really made it anywhere. I learned very quickly that the universe wasn't planning on me walking any red carpets. My memories of childhood are still very pleasant. Both my parents have loved me unconditionally. I have always been their Northstar; the center of their universe. I never experienced any trauma; quite the opposite, my parents were very over-protective and made it their priority to always show me how loved I was and made me feel safe. I mean, talk about over-protective, they were afraid I'd hurt myself learning to ride a bike. That said, I was intrigued to working mostly with trauma cases for my entire career. In all my years of practice, trauma was my specialty. Sexual abuse and addictions was my favorite. I always enjoyed working the most complex cases. Somehow working on the transformation of my client's lives was very rewarding for me. I felt that each person I had the honor to work with, was there to show me another aspect of life; something I clearly had not experienced as a child. As a teenager, I continued reading metaphysical books, hoping to learn as much about the controversial subject as possible. I became a follower and student of Brian Weiss, learning how to do regressions therapy. He is a renowned author and a former Chief Psychiatrist at a Miami hospital who has written several case studies on Past Life Regressions, something I later used in my own practice. Fascinated by the concepts, I continued to dig for a deeper sense of meaning. Nothing convinced me. My impatience grew stronger.

When I was 23 and recently divorced, I became certified in hypnotherapy while still attending Florida International University (FIU), in pursuit of a psychology degree. At the time, both my girls were little babies. Amber was almost one

77

year old, and Gemeny, was turning five. Working with hypnosis changed my life forever. It helps to work with the root of all problems, which reside in the subconscious mind. The last fourteen years have been filled with lessons. Looking back now, I can see how the universe was preparing me for all of this. These tools have been useful, especially during those moments when I feel at times so lost and confused. Sure, I forget sometimes to use them, but, I still have them. I know how to use them. I know how well they work and the fact that these tools are my only saving grace to redeem myself from this place.

However, I acknowledge that there are moments where I seem distant, trapped in the past, constrained by all the memories I still cling to. In theory, I am on a mission of some sort, serving as a link between two very different worlds. An outside world where I learn to figure things out on my own, and this world, where I feel lost and I don't even know where to begin. Was this what I was here to do? Become the bridge that allowed the outside world to awaken by the circumstances that brought us together? It's as if the act of being present made me feel uncomfortable and unfortunate. However, as I look around, I'm reminded of the person I was; starving for growth and committed to always being of service. Certainly, the thought of unresolved karmic debt came to mind. I strongly believe an encounter with another person is a result of some unfinished business we carry from another life. Most occur because of things that remain unsettled. Knowing that I was here for a purpose seemed somewhat like a pending debt that would give rise to a brighter future; one that was less leery and complicated.

There are those whom I have met here that have expressed a constant sense of arrogance and through humor, have camouflaged their fight for self-preservation. Several of the inmates are living double lives, engaging in same gender relationships while getting all primped up on the weekends when their husbands and children visit. Can you blame them? Everyone is so deprived of love in here. Other women speak with pride of their charges, yet, claim to be victimized by the system. It's clear that they are the exception to the rule. In general, there are those who do not belong in here. I'm not saying that if you commit a crime, you should get away with it and not be punished, I'm simply stating that there are other ways to be held accountable. If prison would provide programs for the criminals that focused on their mental and emotional well-being, there wouldn't be people returning to prison. If these programs addressed accountability for their crimes, taught them to discover their true potential and the root of their problems, I would be the first person to support our prison system. It's not like that at all. People in prison get worse. They are incapable to properly channel their emotions and behaviors because there aren't programs that can assist them. Programs that will teach them to have meaningful lives. They are deprived of their primary needs.

I try to resist the temptation of discussing my situation or making it the focus of any conversation with any of the other inmates. Instead, I make a serious effort to focus on their stories so I can document later and I try to understand these women without any judgement. I remind myself that I am here to learn from them. Consequently, it is very easy to see the inner turmoil some of these women are experiencing. In most cases, I'm able to see that what they most lack is love. I'm intentionally trying to imagine what it must be like to live their story, so, I can better understand. Most are empty and have been devoid of love their entire lives. They have suffered rape, abuse, neglect and come from families who are serving time in other prisons too. Some of these women, simply don't know any better. Many have been in the system for most of their lives. They don't know anything else. This is what they know. This is their life story.

In his prayers, Saint Francis of Assisi said, "Lord, make me an instrument of thy peace. Where there is hatred, let me sow love; where there is injury, pardon; where there is doubt, faith; where there is despair, hope; where there is darkness, light; where there is sadness, joy." It is only in giving that we receive. Whether it be from our thoughts, feelings, or our behaviors, our entire life shifts when we are sharing our love with others, even if they are completely unaware of it. This reminds me of Stephanie, an inmate who left Coleman a year earlier, before I arrived. Her story appeared in an article written by Brendan Kirby, of the Press-Register newspaper published in Alabama.

Stephanie had only known John, the guy involved in her case, about a month before she was sentenced to 30 years for crack cocaine charges back in 1990. She was a single mom with four kids, another on the way, and a first-time offender. At the time, she was only 23 years old. John testified against her, alleging that she was doing drug deliveries for him and picking up money. He was rewarded with only a 15-year sentence from the original life sentence for testifying against her. Because of a new law that was passed in 2010, The Fair Sentence Act, Stephanie would soon be going home after serving 21 years. She was 44 years old by the time she was released. She was only one of thousands of federal prisoners who have shared a similar story. I never had the chance to meet her, but, was told she was a very nice person. She was never bitter or resentful for what had happened to her. Perhaps somewhere deep inside she had learned to forgive and accept her circumstances honorably. I always admired the women who had gone through so much and somehow managed, every single day, to put on a happy face. On many occasions, unless you knew someone's story, you would never imagine what they had gone through. Every night I lie down and, before falling asleep, I replay some of the stories I hear in my mind over and over and over again. I pray they would go home to their loved ones. I pray for their freedom and healing. There truly is nothing more rewarding than praying for someone else. It was a selfless act you do without expecting anything in return.

Around 10:30 pm, Ms. P, a woman in our unit becomes terribly ill. She had surgery just a few weeks prior and is having a rough time recovering. A gallbladder procedure; the type of surgery that is outpatient and has a quick recovery. In her case, she appears to be getting worse by the day. She is pale, and her body is fragile; she feels so bad that she barely eats and has been taken to the Medical Unit several times already. She expresses how terribly she has been feeling but they continue to ignore it and send her back to her room.

This evening, Ms. P. becomes incoherent. Her eyes rolling back, and she could barely sit up in her wheelchair. We are all getting ready for count time. Two guards just arrived, but, just a few seconds before they did, one of the women picked up the phone and called a guard over the intercom. 'We are all afraid that Ms. P. is going to die.' When the guards arrived, one of them stood in front of Ms. P.'s fragile body, while another inmate is holding her head up, as it keeps wobbling from side to side. The other guard begins asking who picked up the phone in our unit to page him. When the inmate responded it was her, he interrupts her and tells her she was never to pick up the phone again. He immediately goes downstairs without assisting Ms. P.

He returns, takes the woman who used the phone to page from our unit straight to county jail. It does not matter that this is a medical emergency, Ms. P. is still sitting wobbling her head in her wheelchair without receiving any help. I pray fervently for Ms. P. to survive. I feel so impotent and frustrated by my inability to do anything. If I do, I'll also be sent to the Shu (county jail). I am angry, and I just want to stop this injustice. After what seemed a lifetime, Ms. P. is finally taken downstairs to medical where they will call the paramedics and send her off to the hospital.
I've been tossing and turning all night long. I can't stop thinking how inhumane and unjust this treatment is. It doesn't matter if any of us are ill or dying. It's one of the most desperate feelings in the world to see such injustice right in front of your eyes and I'm not able to do anything about it. It's now been a week since Ms. P. was taken to the hospital. She has finally arrived back to Coleman and has some color in her face, she is no longer frail and pale. She looks alive and is slowly recuperating. It's a relief to see her. It's also a confirmation that miracles do exist. I believe our outpouring of love helped to heal her.

Chapter 4

The prison compound is closed today. It is raining outside, so I lay quietly in bed. A few days ago, Sylvia had purchased an mp3 player to pass the time. She lends it to me so I'm not so bored. Mp3 player in hand I listen to André Rieu swaying to the violin's lamentations. I can't afford to buy my own Mp3 player, so I use Sylvia's instead. It's hard for me to contain the tears again. I feel more capable of flooding the compound than the storm raging outside. I am thinking of Gemeny.

I miss her. I keep thinking of her playing the violin. I'm remembering all of the concerts I have attended. I savor the pride I had felt when I watched her play. For a moment, I close my eyes and imagine what she must have felt as she held the violin in her hands and created such wondrous music. Does she know how proud of her I am, watching her from my dimly lit seat at those concert halls all those months ago? With every tear, I question if I ever expressed how much she means to me. I sigh heavily, too aware that the last four years have been ridden with a bit of animosity and distance. Gemeny is strong-minded and strong-willed. I am the control freak who always wants to be right.

When Gemeny turned 14, we embarked on a challenging, bumpy road. She has always been a good kid, yes, but, she is stubborn as hell. Like her own mother, Gemeny stands her ground from an early age. Yet, I did not acquiesce to her demands easily. I fought back with all of my might. It was a battle that neither of us ever won. Instead, our relationship was consistently bumpy. Looking back, I realize we could have skirted past many of those obstacles. I had once again allowed my ego to dictate my decisions more often than I should have. It took me a long time to realize that a war could only be fought if there are two people involved. In any war, there are always casualties that could have been avoided.

Luckily, there were no deaths in our familial war. I did realize, though, that I was handling it all wrong. Einstein once said, "The true definition of insanity is doing the same thing over and over and expecting different results." Somewhere along the way, I have learned that I just have to let her be. Ironically enough, Gemeny has always had a fascination for butterflies. They personify her desire for freedom and transformation. Like a butterfly, she needs to expand her wings and fly. My job is not to stop her, but, to swing the door wide open so she could fly away. As I lay here, nostalgically listening to the violin tremble in my friends mp3 player, I wish I had discovered this long ago.

It wasn't recently when Gemeny turned 17 years old that I finally understood why she lived her life the way she did. In part, it was her purpose, and, in another, she was teaching me that I could not control her. Why? Because I'm not supposed to. In spite of all the challenges and arguments we experienced during her teenage years, she was a great kid. She always excelled in school, was an avid overachiever, and she always knew where she was headed. She never gave me headaches by using drugs or getting into any legal troubles. She was simply being herself. Looking back now, my biggest regret was trying to control the situations we were facing instead of letting them be. Indeed, I wasted a lot of precious time that now, due to my inopportune circumstances, have been ripped from me.

In this moment I think about her. I wonder what Gemeny is up to. I wonder about time. I wonder about forgiveness. In this moment, surrounded by 165 incarcerated women in my unit, I wonder about life in general. Would I have made the time to reflect as I do now, if I weren't restricted to this itchy mattress and scratchy mp3 player? The meaning of life has changed for me completely and drastically. Friends, family, past, present, and future; all of it is intertwined in my thoughts. Feelings of gratefulness and regret melded together nostalgically. The only thing that separates one thought from the other is a resounding sigh. Gemeny is leaving for college in a few days. Shouldn't I be excited? Just as quickly as I thought this, fear stepped in to answer. The fear of what seems to be justifiable to me: she is just 18 years old in a city that could swallow her up alive. New York City was one of those places that could either make or break you. I lay here gnawing on my lower lip, as I realize that her father would not help her, and I am stuck inside both my head and this 6x10 prison cubicle.

I have no doubt that Gemeny has been noticeably shaken by the sudden and recent changes in her life. She is starting college in a completely different city; one she's only been to visit a few times before. Not to mention, New York isn't the average city. Then there was the fact that I can't be there to help her through this transition, perhaps one of the most important transitions of her life. Yes, I feel an overwhelming sense of guilt; have I failed my daughter when she needed me the most? Amidst that deep sense of remorse, I also feel a twinge of gratitude knowing these trying circumstances have brought us to recognize what we mean to each other. We are both alive and thus able to make up for any lost time in such a way that restores and strengthens us. I close my eyes and feel her near. I smile as I send her all my love, consciously disregarding all my fear. And as I do so, I attempt to connect with her with the purest intentions. Somehow, I know in my heart that all the months away from each other will bring us closer together. Someday, the pain will turn to joy. The tears will dry and the frowns will transform into smiles. I have so much to look forward to. A different life awaits me somewhere outside because I have already begun the transformation inside of me.

Cycles in life are like gestation periods. For instance, before a child is born, they must go through nine months of development inside their mother's womb. In much the same way, a seed must become a stem, then a bud, before reaching the final stage where its petals are open, full of color and life. Time is not as we see it. Time is relative. I believe the universe measures time quite differently from us. Time is nothing more than a process that is necessary and inevitable. Every moment in time is significant as it represents an opportunity that is being manifested, offering us a chance to grow and bring us closer to who we are.

No one can possibly imagine what it's like to find yourself at 36 years old inside a facility that, even though it may not have bars, still keeps me prisoner; confined by ridiculous laws that only benefit those who impose them. To find yourself living amongst women who are filled with a vast array of issues, both psychological and emotional, isn't that difficult for someone with my background, but, to live with them 24 hours a day, is a pain in the ass. The majority of these women fluctuate in their moods. I speculate that many are undiagnosed bipolar. I can't blame them nor judge them, though. Most have been institutionalized after serving many years.

How about me, who should I blame? Griselda for forging my signature? The branch manager who authorized it? Do I blame myself for not asking questions? Was I in here because I agreed to invest with her? Was I here because I needed a break from my extensive work hours and hectic work life? Had Gemeny meant it when she wished I'd go to jail the night we'd gotten into a heated argument just weeks after my indictment? Could it have been all those times I'd felt so unappreciated by Gemeny that I'd ask God to make me disappear? Or was it God punishing me? The questions linger. The answers, on the other hand, are not as forthcoming. It is very provoking to blame someone for my pain. Yet, how would that change anything? Inevitably, there are moments where I wake up - usually on the weekends I know I won't have any visitors - and I wander around while the other women sleep. I leave my unit and head out to the track. Most days every lap across the track I'm enveloped in thought. After my walk, I sit behind the wellness center, close my eyes and ask God, where are you? How could you exist, be so powerful and call yourself merciful while women like me are in a place like this? I take a deep breath and weep, who wants to believe in such a fucked-up God? A God that doesn't care; one that let's this happen. There are even moments when I try reasoning with God: if you really exist, take me away this instant! I challenge His power and, seeing that nothing happens, proceed to tell Him that He doesn't exist. You see, I spat tiredly, you don't exist. You are an asshole. There goes my ego again, can it just shut up for once? I know all too well that God has nothing to do with any of this. It's like that book I read, What God Wants written by Neale Donald Walsch. God wants nothing. He gives us free will so we can design our lives as we see necessary for our growth. We stand today on the brink of a global cultural war.

I've always believed that as humans, we all have free will. I've often read that before we are born, our souls determine a plan for the type of experiences we will endure in our life. We do so in order to help us grow closer to the Light of God. If this is true, I must have been on an exaggeratedly heavy dose of psychotropic meds when I decided that I needed to go to prison in order to get closer to this so-called light of God. If only there was some magical eraser or divine whiteout that I could have borrowed right before the moment of my indictment. How gracious it would be if I could just hit a delete button from that day until the moment I walk out these doors. Would I have learned as much as I'm learning right now, even as I write this? My honest, heart-wrenching response is no. I would not change a thing. As desperate as I feel sometimes, I would not change what's happened. It's my ego who would disagree. I know that all of this is necessary for my personal growth. As brutally painful as this journey may be, it is also purposeful.

All my life I have walked around on automatic pilot with a silk handkerchief wrapped around my eyes. Life wasn't perfect by any stretch, but I have lived a life of my own choosing. I have been blessed with the ability to move past many obstacles and optimistically live a life I desired. I traveled as much as I wanted to, made friends easily anywhere I went. I have a unique name that, when heard, draws a lot of attention; Sheena Eizmendiz. I'd say it has character, represents my eccentric personality and style: overly confident yet humble, sympathetic to others' needs and pain; hungry for life, success, and a thirst for enjoyment. Perhaps what I lack the most is surrendering to the idea that I do not control anything. Since I have worked so damn hard my entire life, I have felt that I have created my own success. I attribute most of my accomplishments to my unwillingness to give up, my drive and persistent attitude to manifest what I desire. Whatever remains from all that grandiosity, I credit God.

I'm such a fool. It is because of God that every time I fall down, I stand right back up only stronger. I am simply the vehicle by which He manifests all His riches. Yet, knowing this, I still fall to my knees in despair, questioning God for allowing me to go through so much pain in order to learn something valuable to my existence.

The realization that I might have deliberately volunteered to be here does not exactly comfort me, but, it does help me a great deal when trying to accept all the things I do not understand yet. Just as I may have chosen to come and experience my time at a prison, so did all the others who were here before, during, and after my incarceration. Granted, it doesn't feel like my soul knows best. I feel like I have taken a detour right off the straight and narrow. I rammed myself head first into a ditch filled with rocks and soiled streams. The stream, dark and stagnant, has no direction, it just flows with a foul smell that often made me scream for help inside of me. That is what it feels like most mornings. Not salvation, not divine wisdom, just screaming inside my chest.

Groaning, I sit up from my bunk and slide into the stiff gray chair next to it. Inside my room, or Penthouse Suite as my friend's often call it, I overhear the woman next to me say, "sometimes this all seems like a dream; like one day I m going to wake up and it's all going to be over." As soon as she finishes her sentence, I think, That's just it, we need to wake up so it could all be over! I was talking about the idea that everything around us is part of an illusion. Reality is nothing more than what we perceive it to be right? In turn forces us to question if reality even exists. What is real anyhow? If this is real, then it really sucks.

Inside Coleman, there are many women who perceive their incarceration as a wonderful occurrence, somehow the conditions and relationships inside the prison are much better than the traumatic lives they had outside of the prison. Of course, some find negativity in everything, spending their time complaining and blaming others for what happened to them. Even if this was somewhat true, their bitterness and their continued attempts to inflict pain on others did not justify or validate the reality of their situation. Reality is subjective. Some of these women are currently working with the FBI to open new cases and incriminate others, mostly brokers and medical professionals. In exchange for names, they will have their sentences reduced. It was like filling your hands with blood without committing the actual murder. Rumor is that Griselda has been working on one such deal in an attempt to lower her sentence at the expense of more innocent associates. I have no way of proving this, nor do I care to. It is enough that I am already here.

Looking around at all the drama, bickering, and gossip reminds me of one of those foreign films directed by Pablo Almodóvar. The kind of film that keeps you captivated but confused at the same time, where the cinematography unexpectedly spins out of control. I have been a huge independent film lover for many years. I used to attend the Miami International Film Festival every year. For one week straight, I had a chance to see the most eccentric films of the year. Ironically, at Coleman I have a front seat view of the drama I'd once only witnessed on screen. Now here it is in front of me and all I want to do is look away. Most of the drama takes place amongst the inmates. There are little communities throughout the compound. You'll find the Cubans sitting together under a tree playing dominos bickering about who won. Then, there are the rednecks and hicks gathered in their own little group by the fence. Further along you'll find the African Americans, who typically hang out outside the units crocheting. They are the majority here. Luckily for me, I get along with everybody. Obviously, I know there are a few who dislike me, but, not for any particular reason. I think it has something to do with the fact that I'm cordial, polite, and mind my own business while at the same time, I'm not here to take anyone's bullshit, whereas, certain women here spend the day gossiping about other inmates. I'm surrounded by a pack of wolves. At every corner you turn, the wolves are gathered together staring and smiling. They look at me like animals salivating right before eating their prey. Thankfully, there isn't any violence at the camp. That said, it is easy to get stabbed in the back by a fellow inmate. It usually turns out to be your own bunkee. Sometimes, it will be very calm for a few minutes when out of nowhere, someone starts shouting or the 'Jump Out Boys' come out searching for contraband. It isn't too difficult to spot the good inmates from the bad ones. The bad ones have really dark energy, it's very strong and easy to recognize. I get this feeling of warning, like a big yellow sign in the road. I always try to follow my intuition and remind myself of where I am. That way, I'm alert and never get caught off guard. After all, I am in prison and not at a resort in the Dominican Republic.

Griselda is walking the compound with a bible underneath her arm. I see her sitting under one of the trees flipping through the pages. Maybe, she is repenting, or, at least she is pretending to be. I don't want to judge or criticize what she did. I know my words and thoughts are powerful and every emotion I feel creates my reality. I look at her walk by after a while, smile genuinely, sometimes I even chat with her a bit, I ask her how her daughter's are doing, then continue on my path. The best thing for me is to leave behind any resentment. Trust me, this isn't always easy. There are moments when I hear her preaching about how unfairly she was sentenced. She'll sit around, victimizing herself every chance she gets. She claims she did not benefit in any way monetarily, she was simply operating a mortgage company. She groans that she does not belong here, that the real crooks are the judges and prosecutors.

I partially agree. It was clear that most of us are here to make someone else rich and powerful. When we oppose in any way, we are sent to county jail. Everything is always a threat. If we don't do this, you are sent to county. If we don't do that, you are sent to county. Shots are given out every single day. Shots are another word for a write up. After a few Shots, you are sent to county jail. More often than not, no shots are given; they'll just send you to county without warning.

Our mail arrives daily at roughly 9:00 pm and it's the highlight of our day. In tonight's mail, I received a notice of hearing for a motion my ex-husband had filed in court to obtain full custody of Amber. I can't say I was surprised. This is his way to make sure he doesn't have to pay any child support. My ex-husband is the product of what I enabled him to become. I recognize that now. He has gone as far as he can to stop providing for his daughters. Months before I self-surrendered, Gemeny called him asking if he could continue giving her the $300 of child support payments while I was in prison. She was just about to move away to New York City. He ignored her plea. After all, when we first divorced, I wanted to prove to him that I was self-sufficient and that I did not need him to provide any child support payments for our daughters. My ego wanted to teach him that the less money in child support he gave me, the more money I would somehow earn in my business. Looking back, I made things way too easy for him. I took away his parental responsibilities by assuming the role of mom and dad. I wanted to be Wonder Woman. I thought I could do it all. Whatever they needed, I made sure to work my ass off so they can have it. No matter what it took. My ego wanted something to prove to him. My ex-husband had remarried the same woman he cheated on me with. I left him the same day I caught him cheating and I filed for divorce 3 days later in court. I wasn't angry at her or him for breaking up our marriage. Our marriage had been dysfunctional for years. In reality, she never came between us, the marriage didn't work from the start. We were both too young to start a family. What the hell were we thinking? We started dating when I was just 15 years old and I got pregnant with Gemeny when I was 18 years old and he was only 21 years old. The relationship was going to end sooner or later. We were both two very different people. I wore the super hero cape and then blamed him for not providing for the kids in the way I expected him to. So, the fact that he isn't helping Gemeny out while I'm in here, doesn't surprise me. This motion he filed isn't any different. I think we screw ourselves up when we set ourselves up with certain expectations. We assume that the other person will do the right thing according to our standards. I take accountability for my role in all this. You can't force someone to do what they don't feel like doing, or, in his case, what he allows his wife to convince him to do. Yes, he did marry that woman, but, I don't know if he did it for love, or, because he doesn't know how to be alone. Honestly, we could have all gotten along quite well all these years. Unfortunately, her insecurities have never allowed us to be a united family and to co-parent our children. I find it so ridiculous. I have never understood what it is she fears. After all, I am the one who filed for divorce. I recognize that we were never ready to be married, let alone, raise a family. We were kids. We had no experience. She has been a huge issue in the life of my daughter, Gemeny. I assume it's because Gemeny reminds her of me so much, that she treats her the way she does. After all, the apple doesn't fall far from the tree, as they say. I tried several times to make amends and see if she would get over her stupid jealousy, but, she simply couldn't. It's torn apart my relationship with my ex-husband because he doesn't see that she is the cause of the issues. It didn't have to be this way. We could have all gotten along great. I am that ex that stays friends with all her exes. I believe that just because a relationship ends, it doesn't mean, we need to end our friendship too. I would have gladly invited them to all my barbeques and even traveled with both of them and the kids. I saw this with my parents. My mom has always gotten along well with my dad's first wife. Why not? Relationships don't always last. Why all the animosity? Gemeny has had to deal with all the rejection from his wife. She has managed to somehow separate my ex-husband not only from her but also from his own family. It's very sad. Someday, I hope he sees this and decides to make amends before it's too late.

It's August 21st, my 37th birthday. I sit down to read my emails. My friend Eddie has written to wish me a happy birthday. He mentioned I should celebrate my life, that today I deserve to celebrate myself regardless of my circumstances. He said I had given so much to others that I should try to enjoy my day. So, I did, or at least I attempted to. I don't hear much from Eddie, quite honestly, I thought he would have come to visit me by now, but, he hasn't mentioned it. I know he is going through his own storm from a recent breakup with his partner, but, I thought I could count on him being here for me. We have been friends for so many years. I miss my friend. I entertain myself by checking my emails several times a day. My beautiful Amber writes to me every single day, it's no surprise to read one of her emails wishing me a happy birthday today. I know both of my kids have been affected by all of this, but, I feel Amber is having such a hard time adjusting to not having me there, especially today. She is living with her dad and step-mother.

Amber is very much an introvert when it comes to her emotions. She likes to observe people and has little to no judgement of them. That doesn't mean she isn't affected by all of this. She and I are very close. She's still a baby in my eyes. Amber hurts in silence. I can almost feel her from afar. I miss her so much. She has always been my little shadow. Wherever I go, Amber follows. I love having her with me. She is incredibly smart and has a heart of gold. I feel that we have been together in other lifetimes. She grounds me. Her energy centers me. She doesn't have to say much, but, just stand near me and I could already feel grounded by her presence. It's hard to explain. She is also very spiritual. Amber has an inclination for the supernatural and spiritual. Perhaps because I always brought her with me to Elizabeth's house for all the full moon ceremonies and Kabbalah classes. She must be suffering tremendously, but, she will never tell me because she doesn't want to concern me. Her dad will never bring her to visit me. She's probably suffering in silence. This is killing me. I won't be there when she starts high school in a few days. Oh my God, she will be a freshman. How quickly time passes. She's such a great kid. My only birthday wish is that I could get the hell out of here and get back to my life, back to my kids. Vicky and Sylvia have come by to get me. It was time for us to go back to the track and do our daily walking ritual. Later today, my friends are planning a little birthday party inside my unit for me. They have cooked my favorite meal, pizza and cake. Coleman style of course. They set a table in the media room, Vicky and Daisy are joining us. They are hiding from the guard since they both live in other units, They are out-of-bounds for being in our unit. It was very nice of my friends to do this for me. Lisa, my bunkee is invited to join us as well. I'm so happy to have all my friends here celebrating my birthday. They make my day very special. After dinner I came up with the idea to write a list of all the positives reason for being here. This is what I came up with:

1. I don't have to be Wonder Woman.
2. There's more time to read.
3. Write my book.

4. Plenty of Me time.
5. No more 10-12 hour work days.
6. I can do nothing all day.
7. Sleep in late if I want to, if I don't, but, I could.
8. Learn that the world goes on without me.
9. Nothing to control.
10. Exercise everyday.
11. Take all the yoga, zumba and art classes I want.
12. Nothing to stress about.

It would never have dawned on me that these are exactly the things I lacked the most in the outside world. This is what it would have been like if I had learned to let go while I was out there; if only I had put away the Wonder Woman costume long ago.

Suddenly, I realize I have done it all out of fear. The fear of what? I don't even know what. A fear that wasn't even justifiable at this point. So many times, I read about the topic of fear, I even preached about it to others, but, all this time I was holding onto it myself. Intellectually, I know letting go is the key to life, but, emotionally or, better yet, the archetype of Wonder Woman strongly believed she had to hold on and control everything. Here I was in a place where I have nothing to control simply because there was nothing to control. Okay, now that I got it, can I go now? That thought permeated my mind all day, but, I know there was still more to learn.

I wake up the next morning still feeling off-track. Shaken by the idea that there really are no absolutes in this world. Everything contained both good and bad. I decide I need to vent. Who better to vent with than Elizabeth? She always had a knack of drawing profound wisdom from within me. Wisdom I could not see at this very instance, but, she recognized in moments of doubt and despair.

Leaning by the phone stand, I dialed her number from memory. The phone rang a few times before she answered. At the sound of her voice, I broke down into tears. I could barely contain myself, submerged in sorrow, anger, and frustration. With her usual calm and poised voice, she says, "You are not a prisoner. You are only imprisoned in your own mind." I continue sobbing like a child, telling her that I can't stand it any longer, explaining to her that the universe had made a mistake, that I can't handle this place. She insists that the universe makes no mistakes, that I had chosen this experience, that I'd forgotten, but, it was a collection of many debts from previous lifetimes. She assures me that I am purifying my soul after having reached what some consider to be, bottom. Prison is the absolute deepest abyss I've ever known. She told me she prays for me everyday. I whimper as I tell her that I can't bear to see so much injustice, so many women being punished and taken from their small children.

Before she could answer though, I had to hang up. It hurts to say goodbye. Her voice comforts me in this dark place.

Placing the phone back on its hook, I race back to my room for the 10:00 am count. As I rush to my cubicle, I hold my breath, wipe my tears and stare at the ground. The guards walk nonchalantly past us, counting. As soon as it's over, I break down once again. I even cry in front of my bunkees, something I swore I would never do. They rush to comfort me. As I sob uncontrollably in their arms, Isa, one of the girls who was part of the Christian group who lived across from my cubicle asks me if I want to talk in private. "We can pray", she adds. The idea of praying was the last thing on my mind, but I agree. Isa is sweet. She is a beautiful person, inside and out. She has two kids and she is here because she decided to go to trial. Luckily for her, she was only sentenced to four years. Most people who go to trial end up serving many more years. Oftentimes, they serve 10-30 years for similar crimes. So, she is very lucky, to say the least.

I feel I need to talk, to vent, to express all the pain that is still lingering inside of me. I am feeling desperate for attention. Here she is in front of me, ready to give me just that. We go to the library inside our unit. It's a small room filled with books and a desk with two chairs. We sit in front of each other, which seems almost too familiar. We talk for almost an hour. I express what my fears are and where all my emotional pain is coming from.

She too, shares some of her experiences on how she got here. She tells me that God has a plan for me. She says she could see I am much more powerful than I imagined myself to be. She tells me that God has me there for a reason and that I have to trust Him above all. I get what she is saying. I just feel so incredibly depleted today. I will go outside to eat, walk a few miles around the track, shower and go to sleep. I feel as if I have no more energy left in me today.

By 5:15 am each morning, the announcements begin: "pill line is open, insulin line is open, Mainline is open." These blaring announcements are made every single day several times a day. It's starting to grate my mind. I find myself constantly annoyed and on edge. Some days are just unbearable. No matter how much I try to entertain myself, I always return to a lingering sense of melancholy into my past. Reminiscing about the foods I used to eat. My stomach is constantly growling most of the day. I don't think I will ever eat another can of tuna when I get out.

These feelings are especially true during weekend visitations. Whether you have one or not, the compound inevitably feels dreary and bittersweet. The majority of the women do not have family visit them. A large amount of these women aren't even from Florida. Their families live in other cities or states, while others have family outside the country! I sit with one of these women and ask her how she ended up so far away from her family. She explains that the camps in her city are overpopulated, so she was bounced from county to county until she finally reached Coleman. She had not seen her children in several years.

The reality behind this is simple: money. It's unreasonable to think families can afford to consistently fly to Coleman simply to sit with an inmate for a few hours. Many of the women in here only see their families once a year! You're considered lucky if your family visits every week. My family cannot visit me often, either. There simply isn't any more money available now that I'm in here. Visitations are so expensive. It costs roughly a few hundred dollars just to drive here from Miami and stay at the nearby hotel. My family depended on me as the breadwinner and now that I'm gone, they can barely make it on their own. I wish I can ask them to come visit me but I can't impose this on them. It is hard for me to accept that I won't be able to see my family every week or even every month while I remain here. It is a five-hour drive from Miami to Coleman. Even still, not one weekend goes by without my heart aching. I wish I could see my daughters, my mother, my father, or my friends, anyone! Unfortunately, this isn't possible. Gemeny is in NYC now, Amber is with her dad, and he won't make any effort to bring her here. All I have are emails and a few calls I make each week. I don't even have enough money to eat in here, I have to put the money to pay for the phone calls and emails, to the side, every time I get my commissary money deposited. As the weekend slowly comes to an end, I find myself growing sadder and sadder. It's a combination of anger and grief. I'm left paralyzed by it.

Moreover, I'm paralyzed by the fact that Vamp has abandoned me here. It's now been a few months since I arrived when he dropped me off at the door. We both cried together at the sight of me being left at the steps of a prison and he turned around and left. I have sent him letters, but, no response. He hasn't come to visit me. I've even mailed him the visitation form several times. We had a bumpy ride the last month or so before I self-surrendered, but, I could never imagine myself going through this experience without him. I know we were both so stressed out with all that was happening. We even said some really hurtful things to each other. We had never expressed words like those at the time. My heart is shattered by his abandonment.

That's not who we are. He has always been my rock. The man I have loved with every bone in my body. How could he not be here for me now? I think about him daily. I go out to the track and cry while I run as I remember him. It's like a hole I have in the center of my chest. I talk to Sylva about him often. I tell her the story of how we met and the relationship we have had all these years. She tries to comfort me by telling me that this may be the best thing for both of us. We have always been there for each other. There wasn't a day that went by that we didn't speak several times a day. We had such an incredibly strong bond. I have never loved anyone the way I have loved him, aside from my kids of course. I desperately needed him now more than ever. He left me here like he was dropping off a FedEx package. I'm so torn with this. There are so many things I wish to tell him, but, I can't. I'm too proud. He should be reaching out to me at least by sending me a letter. Should he? I'm the one in prison. I'm sure the stress of me being in here is taking a toll on him, on everyone.

I wonder if having him to talk to or being able to see him, would actually make this experience better on both of us. I sometimes feel that I really need him through all this more than anyone else. He could lift me, if only he knew. Words simply cannot describe how lost I feel not to have him throughout all this. He brought me solace and a comfort that few people in my life could give me. Looking at his green eyes brought me peace and kept me grounded. Maybe in time, I will understand why this is happening to us.

Without fail, every weekend I see women combating their own grief and sadness, too. I see the inmates walk out of the visiting room following visitation hours with tears welled up in their eyes. Their pain is evident in every labored step they take away from their loved ones. During visits, I always see children of all ages. Some women have three or four kids no older than ten! My heart goes out to them. I ask the universe to please help them to return their mothers home. Sometimes, I start feeling so powerless and so helpless; I break down and cry. I want to help them so badly. It's one of the most frustrating feelings of my life.

I know I'm not here to save these women, I can't. I know that I'm here to learn about myself. I have a lot of time to reflect. Certainly, more than the reasons that led to my sentencing, I am here for a bigger purpose. I am growing like I never have before. For one, I've stopped sweating the small stuff. Sometimes, I joke that I'm at Coleman on a workaholic rehab program. I used to work very long hours. My entire life revolved around work even when I wasn't working. I had poured my heart and soul into my career, many times at the expense of my family. I'm sitting outside by a tree, remembering all the moments I'd interrupted my time with my daughters to attend to work. We'd be in the middle of conversation when suddenly I'd get a text or call from one of my employees at my office. Without hesitating, I'd make that the priority, explaining that it was work. I had to call and see how things were going. Amber complained and would say, "You care more about your clients than you do about me." I'd smirk, then roll my eyes, dismissing her as dramatic. I would remind her that it was because of the office that I could provide her with all the things she wanted. That was always my excuse.

Looking back now, I used that excuse a thousand times. The worst part about it is that I believed it. After all, as a single mom with very little financial help from my ex-husband, I felt an obligation to providing my girls with everything I could possibly give them. When it came to school, I hired tutors, private instructors, musical classes and instruments. I paid off their Florida Prepaid tuition by the time they were 11 years old. I also worked hard for a lifestyle of travel, dining out all the time, since I was such an awful cook, and maintained a comfortable home. At the time, I didn't want my kids to lack anything. I produced the living conditions that most single parents wouldn't be able to. They never lacked anything, not in the material sense. At least not until now.

What they lacked the most was having me around. A mom who was more present. I was never home by five or even six o'clock in the evening. For most of my career, I worked Monday through Saturday, 7am to 7pm. I did that for roughly 14 years, maybe a little more. What was I thinking? Sure, my kids were enrolled in activities like dance, piano classes, belly dancing, and karate, but, I never stuck around to watch them perform. I'd drop them off and run back to the office and work an extra 30-45 minutes instead of staying with them and enjoying the moment. With this in mind, I thought I was doing a great job as a mom. I was, after all, providing them with these classes all while juggling a business that was steadily on the rise.

In retrospect, I realize now I had a problem. I was a workaholic and didn't know it. I made myself believe that I had to live, breathe, and eat work in order to provide my family with what they needed. My ambition and hunger for success went above and beyond. In my mind, it was never enough; not the fact that I had a beautiful office with the most amazing staff.

Not the money, not the merit, not even the occasional TV interviews or the possible reality show we were in the middle of filming before my indictment, or, my weekly radio show on Y-100. Nothing was ever enough to satisfy my vision of where I wanted to be in life. The irony is, even while I recognize how fortunate I was to have gotten so far, I wasn't really enjoying any of it. I was overwhelmed and overworked, consumed by responsibility and commitments. If it wasn't an event I had to attend, it was something else work-related, be it a meeting or networking dinner. When I think back to how I felt while driving home after work so many late evenings, I clearly see how exhausted I was. I had not only dealt with the business aspect of the office all day long, but, I had spent a good ten hours trying to resolve and address other people's emotional and mental issues as their coach and hypnotist. Every single client had a different story and goal I had to achieve. My job was to help them peel off the layers and help them find a solution and create a change that would ultimately bring happiness and fulfillment to their lives. But, what about my life? The price of doing so was very high and I was blinded by the ambition of being the best at what I did.

No matter how exhausted and depleted I felt, I was addicted to my career. Obviously, I lacked a great deal of balance. Don't get me wrong, I worked out often. I got into running a few races each month, a newly found hobby I enjoyed very much. I worked hard, but, I also played hard. There were the happy hours and dinners with friends, which probably happened once or twice a week. During the summer, it was the beach just about every single weekend. I loved spending time with my friends, Mercedes and Rony. The kids would always come with us on the boat, so, it was nice family time. Amber never missed an outing. She tagged along pretty much wherever I went, even to the office. Poor thing would be bored out of her mind. I'd order her food, give her my laptop and forget she was there. I was too consumed by my ambition to work and be successful. Whenever she'd see me walk in and out of a session, she'd ask, "Mom, when are we leaving?" I'd always respond, "Soon. I'm busy." Hours would go by and, before I knew it, we'd have spent the entire day at the office.

Some Saturdays, I'd stop by the office in my workout clothes, convinced it would be a simple 10-minute stop. A few hours later, I'd still be at the office working away. My assistants and interns would encourage me to leave and enjoy my Saturday. Amber would be exhaustingly calling and texting me to come home having left her behind waiting for me. It was easier to come up with an excuse and continue doing the same thing than to stop and change it. Besides, in my mind, I wasn't doing anything wrong, I was attending to my business affairs and providing for my children.

Given the opportunity now, I'd work less and enjoy my family and personal time a lot more. While in prison, I've realized that it's the simple things that matter. Gemeny once told me she wished I had been a soccer mom. She wanted a mother that either didn't work, or, worked a part-time job. The kind of mom who drove a van, not an Audi like the one I had. One who carpooled all the kids to soccer practice right after school around three in the afternoon. This so-called soccer mom stayed to watch the kids play soccer and then take them all to eat ice cream afterwards. More than a soccer mom, I resembled a chicken without a head, one who worked long hours to earn the type of income that would allow her kids to play soccer if they wanted to. I often coordinated with another mom, usually a soccer mom, to pick up or drop off my kids at practice. Meanwhile, I'd rush through traffic to pick my daughters up, drop them off at home, and rush back to the office. On the way, I'd buy them food, or leave them enough money to order in. It was non-stop; this ordeal went on for years. Somehow, I became a slave to my business without realizing it. I was indeed feeding my ego to the fullest. I was an idiot. I guess this is what it took for me to acknowledge this. Damn, couldn't the lesson be less brutal? I'm going into our small library located inside our unit.

I just overheard an inmate's story on how she ended up here. She is telling another inmate in our unit. I begin speaking briefly to her once her friend leaves. I tell her that I like her vision board displayed in her room. Oh man, I used to offer workshops on vision boards when I had my practice. Each year I would gather a group of 50-60 people and teach them to use a vision board to stay focused on specific goals. I love vision boards, I tell her. I must confess that each year I created my own. She said she too believed in vision boards and that they really worked. She's here in the library looking for a book about strong-willed children and needs to see if there are any pictures that she can use on her vision board. I ask her how her search was going. She looks a little puzzled.

Apparently, she's been searching for these pictures in all the magazines she has come across today and hasn't found much. We soon got onto the topic of why she was sentenced again. She has already served 23 years in prison and has another 9 to 10 years to go. She was sentenced to a total of 32 years, charged with a drug dealing conviction. Her ex had been caught dealing and, in an attempt to reduce his sentence, pinned what he was doing on her. He said she knew all along and that she was part of it. Knowing she was innocent, she refused to accept a plea bargain the prosecutor was offering her to serve only 2 years in prison. Instead, she decided to take her defense to trial as recommended by her attorney and prove she was innocent. Sure enough, she was found guilty and sentenced to 32 years. My God, I'm 37-years old. Can you imagine? That's pretty much my entire life existence. I just stare at her with nothing to offer. What do I say? I'm sorry? I take a deep breath and walk out letting her know that I will let her know if I see any of the magazines or books she's looking for. I express how admirable she is and thank her for the conversation.

It is stories like these that tear my heart to pieces and cause me despair. She is a positive and strong-willed African American woman who, even though her life has been crushed and stolen from her for the past 23 years, she is still planning on opening up an organization to help young kids get out of trouble. Here is a remarkable woman in front of me with no hate or anyone to blame, just sincere trust in God. She doesn't have any bitterness in her heart. Only love and light shines through her. I will write down her story and share it with the world. I can't forget to mail some of my manuscripts out today. God save me if they search my locker and just so happen to read this stuff. I make sure that every couple of days, I mail out the manuscripts to Mel. He used to be one of my assistants at the office. He's keeping them for me and will drop them off at my parents' house, so I can organize all the manuscripts and eventually publish my book once I am released. He's just going to die when he reads these stories. Mel is a really soft-hearted guy. He will melt. God, I miss my people. I miss my Mel. I miss my Bianca as well. Bianca had been my assistant for over five years. She started out with me when she was only 18 years old. She was my right and left hand at the office. Bianca grounded me and kept me organized. I love her like family. I think about all my staff often. My office was my home. I really loved being there with everyone. If ever given the opportunity to have an office again, I would never do it the same though. I don't think I will ever work at the expense of being free. The fact is that I was imprisoned to my work. I can't deny the truth.

An inmate fell off the top bunk while sleeping at night. This happened roughly around 1:00 am. Remarkably, only few of us heard it. I was sound asleep. The woman rolled over to the edge of her top bunk and fell off. Her friends awakened by the noise and her screams for help. They immediately call the guard, walk her down to medical. Since it was roughly 1:00 am and medical Is not open at this time, they ask her to return to the unit. Alone and in great pain at this point, she walks back to her bed where she cries all night. I can't sleep. I don't think any of us can fall asleep just listening to her cry. When I saw her return back to our unit, I wanted to rush out and kick the guard in his balls. He doesn't deserve any less. How inhumane can he be? This woman is in agonizing pain. At 6:00 am, she goes downstairs to medical in visible pain and little energy left in her to even walk. It wasn't until around 10:00 am, nine hours after the incident, that the paramedics are called. She broke her arm, dislocated her shoulder when she hit her head with the edge of the locker, so, she also has a concussion. Why the hell didn't they do this last night? My God, the cruelty is just unbelievable. No wonder there have been over 37 accidental deaths between 2011-2012 due to medical negligence inside prisons. These people have no regard for us. We are irrelevant to them. During these times, I desperately try to remind myself that none of these things are happening by coincidence. I had chosen to be here, since I believe we are co-creators of everything that happens to us, maybe, I wanted to be a part of this from the inside to better understand what is happening in our prison system. To be more compassionate and learn to accept that each of us has a very personal reason for being here, one that is beyond any of the crimes we were charged with.

I too sleep in a top bunk. I'm a little concerned that I may fall off while sleeping after what happened to her. Shit, I better be careful. The worst part of her story is the fact that she had requested her case manager to move her to a lower bunk several times, but, they ignored her. She even had a medical pass explaining that she had to sleep on a lower bunk due to severe vertigo.

Unfortunately, this was not surprising to any of us. There are many women here diagnosed with cancer and AIDS and they are not receiving the proper treatments. They are all told that there isn't enough money in the budget to provide them with their meds. There's an inmate who has been taken to the hospital to have heart surgery. She was given a pacemaker. It has been two months since her surgery and she still hadn't seen a cardiologist for a follow up. We will find out, sooner or later, if the pacemaker worked or not. In other words, if the poor woman's heart stops, that pretty much is the indication that it isn't working.

There are hundreds of such stories at Coleman. Some are evidently worse than others. It all feels surreal. Had someone told me about this happening inside our prisons, I would probably put into question what they are saying. You have to see this, to believe it. Society is blind to many things. In fact, if anyone of us are caught disclosing information from this place, we will be sent to the county jail.

Our lives in here feel like some sort of movie. Women often have affairs with other women. It is full of drama and suspense. Everything is unpredictable. Each guard treats us differently from the next. Some are pretty easy going, while others take any opportunity to nourish their narcissistic tendencies by treating us as if we are worthless pieces of shit. There are only a few guards and staff people that I consider kind hearted.

Most of them don't care for any of us. They don't see us as humans, they see us as numbers. They are so disrespectful and unkind. I can't understand why they feel the need to treat us this way. Very few of them treat us with any regard or respect. Lucky for me, my case manager seems to be a little more down to earth and always addresses me with respect. He'll always answer any questions without treating me like I'm any less than he is. He has a different energy from the rest of them. There simply isn't any excuse for them to treat us like they do. I mostly feel sorry for them, knowing that they are only projecting their unhappiness onto us. Surely, they too have to be miserable and in a lot of pain to even work here.

Rarely do any of the guards or unit managers follow the handbook containing all the rules and regulations. However, if the inmates don't follow it, we are either given a shot or sent to county jail. I am convinced that a first grader has written Coleman's ridiculous policies. It's quite sad to see this is a legal form of money laundering in this country. There is no valid reason to have more than half of us serving time in the camp.

Someone in power breaks the law and gets away with it? Heck, the NSA breaks the law every day. It's no secret that they are listening to all our conversations. The whistle has been blown by several NSA employees multiple times about this. This is illegal. They claim it's for our safety. I call it legal fraud. It's all such bullshit.

I've only had a handful of good memories while at Coleman. Most are during an inmate's release. Those last few days before we get to walk out and return to our families are both joyful and sorrowful. We are happy for all those who are leaving, but, we also know that every time a woman leaves, it only means five more will be replacing her. That's just the way it is I guess.

The days drag on no matter how much we try to keep busy and entertained. I go check my emails approximately 20 times a day in hopes that someone has written. I keep busy, but, it's so darn hard to fill in my days. I'm just glad today I am having visitors come see me. "OK, how do I look?" I ask my friend Jackie. She has been here for about four years of her six-year sentence. Jackie admits to the crime she was charged with but like most people here, it was a money crime. She is a really nice person. We live in the same unit. She is married, but, her husband is a prick. He never comes to visit her. What a small world, it turns out we have a friend in common on the outside. We get along great. On weekends when neither one of us has any visitors, we go out to the track and walk our buns off. Jackie works in the garage and she gets to drive a car, which is the biggest privilege. She actually gets to leave the compound and drive around it. We agreed that today she will sneak up after lunch and I will hop in her car and she will take me for a drive around the entire compound, so I can see the other prisons in the area. It's so awesome, but extremely risky of me to do this. Unlike Jackie, I have no authorization to leave the compound. I just want to take a look at what is around us. She is driving me to the post office within our compound, the maximum prison, the medium, all around the camp to the other neighboring prisons too. It's been a few months since I had sat in a car. I feel free for a whopping 10 minutes. It's a quick joy ride but so worth the feeling. My friends Vicky and Sylvia are telling me that I'm crazy for doing this, I could get a Shot or worse, be sent to county jail if I'm caught. I know they are right, but, screw it, It's so nice to be able to leave this shit hole, if only for a moment.

Like me, Jackie doesn't get weekly visits. Today, my friends Mercedes, Rony and Yasmin are coming to visit me. They are bringing Amber. It's been so long since I've seen her. Amber sends me pictures of her dance competitions. She looks so beautiful. It's a shame Gemeny can't come, she is currently living in Boston. I suppose NYC didn't quite work out for her so she decided to move there instead. Jackie is assuring me that I look fine. I don't ever wear makeup or fix myself up unless I have visitors. I am always outside sweating on the track, so, what's the point. I probably reflect how I feel anyway. I don't care to look pretty in prison.

Mercedes is one of my craziest friends. She is insanely funny and embarrasses people with her very unorthodox jokes. I've been friends with them since our kids were really small. We're having a really nice time together today. They get to see what this camp looks like. Well, from the screened patio area outside the visiting room. At least I get to spend some time with them and I'm so grateful they brought Amber. I miss her so much. I don't want to let go of her. I wish they can all take me with them in Rony's big SUV. He drives a huge Tahoe. They should be able to hide me in there. I have introduced them to all my friends. Everyone already knew about them. I have told them how crazy Mercedes is. She says things that are always inappropriate and out of character, but, somehow, she gets away with it. She is funny as hell. It is nearing the time for them to go and I have no clue when I will see them again. This is so painful. This is the part I hate the most.

Chapter 5

March 2012

My attorney is advising me to plead guilty. At first, I refuse. I kick and scream like a four-year old, rebelling from the idea. I can't believe I am being expected to plead guilty for a crime I have not committed. I am heartbroken. I feel immensely angry at him and could not justify his recommendations. The idea of pleading guilty to a crime I have been fighting for over four years prior to my indictment, is devastating. My attorney thoroughly explains that the prosecutor has "evidence" against me. Apparently, they claim that I have benefited from the crime that Griselda has committed. They are stipulating that I was part of her crime. This is so fucking insane. I only purchased my residential home and an apartment as an investment with her. Regardless of all the years of work on this case, with my first attorney, and regardless of the fact that we had proven, in front of a judge, she had forged my signatures and stole my identity, it did not matter. I am already guilty in their eyes.

I am learning quickly, in the federal system, everyone is guilty. I would later understand why. To top it all off, I am informed that Griselda has said that everyone in our case was always aware of what she was doing. I am bound to lose no matter what.

All of this is so unsettling. In civil court, a few years earlier, my civil attorney had proven, with the help of a signature specialist, my signatures were forged on all the closing documents for all of the properties she purchased. What the hell did I spend four years fighting this case for? I was a victim of identity theft and forgery and now I find myself sitting across from my attorney asking me to take the plea. Is he nuts? I'm leaving his office feeling angry, lost, and in despair. I can't understand the justice in the law. There simply isn't any. My attorney just called me and asks me to return a few days later to see if I have made a decision about taking the plea. After much thought, and having seriously considered my options, I decide to accept the plea, against my will. "If you don't plead guilty, they'll sentence you to fifteen years in federal prison." I bow my head and weep. I know I don't have a choice.

My attorney assures me I'm not making a mistake, but, if I still want to go to trial, he would represent me. That's when I understood that he was trying to convince me to plead guilty, so his job would be finished. He knew how it worked. After all, he had been a federal attorney for almost thirty years now. A few hours later, he calls me in his office, so I can sign the plea. Before he hands the paper over to me, he mentions that the prosecutor was giving me an offer. I sit across the conference table from him. He goes on to tell me that if I take the offer, I could get a reduction for cooperation.

Little did I know how incredibly repulsive the offer would be or how these so called offers actually work.

"All you have to say is that Jacob knew all along what Griselda was doing," he explains. My jaw drops. I stare at my attorney coldly. Hell no. I retorted, 'my integrity is not for sale. How could I say such a thing when Jacob had been a victim like me?' Tears run down my face. I am appalled at what I have just heard. How could the prosecutor ask this of me? I decide to grab my purse and leave his office at once.

A week later, I am called in to meet with my attorney, again. This time, he has another offer. "Your last offer", he says righteously. He says that the prosecutor wasn't giving me any more offers if I decline. So when I asked what it was, a list was placed in front of me with all the names of the pending defendants in my case. Once again, if I point out any names and say they knew what was going on, I would get a reduction in my sentence. I simply cannot do it. I would be selling my soul to the devil. First and foremost, I don't know most of the people on this list. Honestly, the ones whose names were familiar to me are only about 4 out of the 20. I wonder if they have given all the defendants this list, this very same offer. I wonder if they have taken the offer to further incriminate me, so they can get a reduction on their sentences. Even with the building doubt, I could not bring myself to do it. That's not me; that's not how I am programmed. Once again, I push the list towards my attorney and growled, "I don't want any more offers. Tell the prosecutor he can stick this list up his ass." I just can't get over the fact that I am being bribed to lie. Apparently, that's how the federal system works. At this point, I now know who the real corrupt criminals are and it sure as hell isn't me.

A few minutes later, I walk out in tears. What kind of justice system is this? Everything is a game in this country; one big, corrupt federal game. In the end, there would only be one winner and it would always be them. My attorney phoned me a few days later to ask if I had changed my mind and decided to cooperate with the prosecutor. I understand he is just doing his job however, I am nauseated at the entire thing. It's repulsive to see that this is how the law works.

A few weeks later, I am scheduled for my plea hearing. Here I am on my way to plead guilty to a crime, I swear, I did not commit. Vamp accompanies me, but, he isn't allowed to go into the courtroom. He has to wait outside the federal building. He is obviously nervous and is trying to keep me from noticing. In the courtroom, it's just my attorney, the prosecutor, and a few others. I sit on a chair next to my attorney, inside a large, cold courtroom.

The prosecutor goes over my charges; we agreed that by pleading guilty, they would drop two of my charges, neither of which made any sense.

One charge was for bank fraud. However, my signatures were forged, and I was completely unaware of all the lines of credit that were being pulled by Griselda. The other charge was for accepting gifts. How was I supposed to know the gifts she gave me were linked to a crime I was completely unaware of? Was I supposed to know that all those birthday's and Mothers' Day gifts were all associated to her embezzlement? I had no way of knowing. None. This is ridiculous.

Today, I am taking a plea for conspiracy to commit bank fraud. I will never forget how I feel when asked by the judge how I plead. I look down and heaved a breath. I have trouble responding. I feel the gaze of my attorney upon me as I look up and plead guilty. The words feel like pure salt inside my mouth. It is surreal, as if I am watching a horror movie, the kind you skip past as you toggle through the channels because you know you are bound to lose sleep if you watch it. As we begin finishing up, I stand and approach the prosecutor and shake his hand. You are making a big mistake. He looks at me in amazement and walks away.

Vamp and I head back home; I'm now officially guilty. In reality, I was guilty a long, long time ago, I just didn't know it. My sentencing is just a few months away. As time passes the only thing I could think of is my family. How will they make it if I'm imprisoned. I am the bread winner. The head of household, as they call it.

While I wait to be sentenced in the weeks that follow, I try diligently to be strong and focused. Once again, I find myself visiting every psychic I could find. I am told by these psychics that I will not go to prison. They claim to be 100% certain they do not see me behind bars. Just about every psychic I visited said this except one, an 81-year old clairvoyant, the aunt of my friend, Eddie. She quietly announces that I am going to prison while rocking herself in her chair. She is telling me to stop spending my money visiting tarot readers. The old lady has "diarrhea of the mouth", as my friend Eddie often says. She is confident that it is in my path. I am going to prison no matter what I do. I try desperately not to believe her and continue on my quest. In search of more answers and false promises from psychics.

At the time, Vamp and I become a lot closer than we had in years. He continues to support me throughout this nightmarish ordeal. One night, we were sexually involved. It had been a little over two years since the last time we had been intimate. This opens up a can of worms. I find myself reliving very powerful emotions; emotions I am not aware I have not buried. However, I have done a good job of disengaging. Vamp has been my greatest love. We lived together for several years and had broken up about seven years ago. Throughout all these years, I still love him. He means a lot to me. We have a very special relationship. We make sure to always be here for each other, unconditionally. Getting involved with him is not a good idea, be it that I am so awe-stricken about all that is happening, and I've now created a false sense of hope. I am vulnerable and it's easy for me to think that this may lead us to getting back together somehow. We continue spending a lot of time together. It feels safe and very familiar. Each encounter is deeply felt. We have shared an undeniable connection for many years and I need him now more than ever.

The day of my sentencing arrives. Vamp, my parents, Gemeny, my friend Eddie, and my intern, Zunamy, are all accompanying me to support me. They are here to pray with me. Knowing my friends and family are here brings me some peace of mind. Gemeny holds my hand while we wait for my name to be called. I try to remain very positive. Deep inside, I am convinced that since my ex-fiancé had been given credit for time served, surely, I would be granted the same. He has already been sentenced. After all, we pretty much had the same case. We had discovered the forgeries, the lines of credit, and all this mess together.

My name is being called. My attorney and I sit in the "hot seat" together. The seat that burns your ass once you are issued your sentence. My attorney makes his recommendations to the judge. He tells her that if she were to sentence me, then he recommended I receive four to six months of house arrest with probation as the maximum penalty. He goes on to make comparisons between my ex-fiancé and I, explaining we had the same charges and, what's more, he had a real estate license, yet she credited him with zero time in prison, no probation, no restitution, not a single thing. The prosecutor stands up and objects, reminds her that I had been involved in a $40 million crime. He mutters that the judge would create a disparity in the court amongst the pending defendants if she sentenced me as my ex-fiancé was sentenced. The prosecutor ends his speech with the recommendation that I receive the maximum penalty of 21 months in prison.

Less than a second has passed, the judge announces that she has reached a decision. She quickly discloses that I am issued the maximum sentence for my crime: 21 months in prison. It will be a split sentence where I will be serving 14 months at a federal prison along with seven months of house arrest, three years of probation, 200 community service hours, and $321,000 in restitution that I have to pay to the federal government. Fuck!

My forehead drops to the table. The only feeling I have is numbness. Numbness that envelopes my entire body. An inner voice keeps saying to me, wake up, this is a dream. I can't lift myself up to look at my family and friends; they have already been escorted outside filled with tears in their eyes. It is the beginning of an internal nightmare for all us. I am immediately taken to the

U.S. Marshal's office for processing. Just like that, my life has changed. In one split second, it is all different now. I'm not just a felon, I am also a soon-to-be prisoner. As I walk to the U.S. Marshal's office, I have flashbacks to my indictment a few months earlier. I can't speak, all I could do is cry. I am hurting for my parents and my daughters. I'm not afraid for me, because I know I will survive this. I am angry with God; I feel betrayed. My anger and pain are one and the same.

Once processed, I walk back to the building where my family awaits. They are all in tears and broken hearted. My dad cannot look at me. He is falling apart deep inside, but, he doesn't want me to see him like that. I hug my daughter, Gemeny, and everyone else who has been here to support me. Surely, I will never forget the way I am feeling. How could this happen? I ask this question a hundred times in my head while we begin to walk outside the federal building. Over and over again, I keep running the entire experience in my mind. Somebody wake me up, please!

All of my friends keep calling and texting me to hear the news. They were all praying for me in hopes that I would only be sentenced to house arrest. I am torn inside. After dropping off my family, Vamp drives me to Elizabeth's house. She is the one person I desperately need to see. I need to look her in the eyes and have her explain how the universe has just failed me. Why is the universe causing me this pain.

I arrive at her doorsteps in tears. She hugs me and says that everything will be fine. She welcomes us inside. She tells me that I had to go to prison to help many people. I argue with her that I had spent 14 years of my career devoted to helping people. She says that this time, it would be different. She insists I have to go there and help them from the inside. I continue to argue with her, I will gladly offer my services to anyone who has ever been incarcerated free of charge, but, I did not deserve to go to prison for a crime I did not commit. Elizabeth looks at me and whispers softly, "you wanted this. You just don't remember." There is always something about the way she says things that resonates deep down inside. The past few days have been incredibly emotional in ways I cannot describe. I continue working and using work as an escape.

Vamp and I continue to spend more intimate times together. He has been very protective. He doesn't allow me to fall into a depression by consistently remaining by my side. I spend many nights with him, bonding deeply and intimately like we used to do years ago. It is only normal, I suppose. It feels special, and indescribably healing to be by his side at this time. We don't have to exchange many words. We are both hurting from all of this. We have a very unique connection. He is what one would call, my soulmate. He is still the man I loved long after we split up.

Chapter 6

September 2011

I figured while my client is in the room under hypnosis, I would slip out for a second to use the restroom. As I open the door, two FBI agents appear at the front desk. Just as suddenly as they appear, they announce, "We're here to speak with your employees." I stare at them in stunned silence. "About what? No. No. No, I have an attorney." I let the silence linger as I try to gather my thoughts. I hadn't heard from my attorney in nearly a year. My legs are shaking and my heart is pounding. I snatch the phone from my assistant and dial my attorney's number. She immediately picks up and reassures me I have nothing to worry about. She was away handling a federal case in New York City, but, would get back to me once she returns. All the while the FBI agents staring at me coldly, trying to intimidate me, they succeeded. "We'll come back." They left just as suddenly as they arrived.

A few days later, my attorney phones me and asks me to come in to speak with her as soon as possible. Shaken, I'm driving over to her office in silence. I don't want any music on, I don't want to call anyone while I'm heading there, I just want to focused on my thoughts right now. I have a knot in my throat. I don't know what to expect. Upon arrival, she sits me down and says, "I have bad news." My heart falls on her carpet. I'm immediately overwhelmed with fear.

She explains that I am going to get indicted, along with 19 other people. Taken aback, I begin to cry quietly. She stares at me indifferently before barking, "I don't know why you are crying." I freeze at her response. I look up from my lap, "What do you mean? How could this happen?" She pulls out her federal book of guidelines and coldly explains, "they're going to arrest you, or, you can surrender. Most likely you are looking at about a year in a federal camp." She states this as if she was preparing me for a vacation in the Maldives, her tone flat and nonchalant. There isn't any empathy or compassion in her voice. Yet, just a few days ago, she had assured me that everything was fine; that the case had been dormant and that I had nothing to worry about.

I still recall our last conversation almost a year earlier, when she told me that no news was good news. She hadn't heard anything from the prosecutor and had gone as far as to reassure me that they may never get to the case because they had hundreds of files to work on. Sitting in her office then, I immediately refuse her offer to surrender. I tell her I would never do such a thing. I was innocent, goddamn! I cry some more before she says, "You need to stop crying. This is what it is and you are getting indicted." I feel my world collapsing with every breath I'm taking.

For the past few days I have been an emotional wreck. All I could do is cry. I stopped eating, sleeping, and nearly stopped breathing. Fear has taken over my mind and body. So I have decided to go on a spiritual search hoping to get some answers. Making sure that my so-called guides and angels haven't abandoned me, I go to every tarot card reader, psychic, spiritual guru and clairvoyant I could find in Miami. If I am asked to wake up at 3:00 am for the next 21 days to meditate, then I am up every day at 3:00 am to meditate. If asked to light 100 candles and pray to the kabbalistic angels, I litter my house with every possible candle I could find. Whatever it is I'm asked to do at this point, I am following. I'm not even questioning it. I just need answers and I need to feel that the universe is with me. I am desperate for answers.

When I consult some of these spiritual people, I am told that because I am innocent, I will not serve any time in prison. The spirits being channeled confirm this time and time again by telling me, "You will not be going to prison." In most readings, the person channeling the information has been very accurate when pinpointing my legal problems and the fraud committed by Griselda. They tell me she is to blame for everything. They explicitly detail about everything that is currently happening. One psychic even gave me the name of the person involved: She said, Griselda framed you. She said I had been betrayed and that this individual would lie through her teeth to save her skin, but, not to worry, I would be safe. I have spent the last few weeks making appointment after appointment, looking for answers.

I hear a loud pounding. Am I dreaming? I must be dreaming or maybe it's just another nightmare? At around 5:30 am, I am awakened by a loud pounding on the front door. I lay my head back on my pillow. I hear that pounding again and this time, someone is shouting out loud: "Open up! FBI!" I sit up in my bed, wondering if I'm having another nightmare. I have spent the last few nights going in and out of sleep because I keep having nightmares. I lay back down slowly, when I hear the shouting continue: In the other room, my daughters are hosting a sleepover with some of their friends. There is no school tomorrow, so I agreed to have a few friends stay over for the night.

I bolt out of bed and run to the living room, where I find Amber, hunched over in tears. I look at her, swallow my own tears, and grab her firmly by the shoulders, "I'm going to be fine." At that moment, Gemeny runs to the door and looks through the peephole. I'm afraid they will break the door down and knock her down with it. It's all happening so quickly. It is indescribably surreal. Swallowing the lump in my throat, I push Gemeny out of the way and open the door.

They rush in, pull me outside and ask if I have any weapons. There are about six or seven agents all armed with huge guns pointing at me and there is a woman from the Department of Children and Families with them too. They immediately turn me around and handcuff me. I begin to yell over my shoulder, "there are kids here!" They ask me how many. I am so shaken by the experience, I begin to shout, "Three! No, there are three kids. Wait, maybe five, six, seven! I don't fucking know. Immediately, they bring me back inside my house to change my clothes and tell me I cannot speak to the kids. As they do so, I look at both of my daughter's eyes and freeze. The fear, confusion, and horror is clearly written on their worried expressions. Ignoring them, the FBI agents shoved past me, seven following swiftly behind. They drag me behind them and only two females take me to my room. I am in shock. I look over at Gemeny as they push me into the room and yell, "Call Elizabeth and Vamp now!" Inside the room, the two female agents sit me down. They aren't rude or aggressive with me. They could clearly see that I have never experienced anything like this before.

With the handcuffs still on, I am allowed to get dressed. It's quite an ordeal to get my sweatpants on and brush my teeth with just one hand. All the while I keep thinking of my daughters faces. Amber is so scared, both for herself and for me. Gemeny is a bit more calm, but, nonetheless, she is also terrified.

I sat down with the girls a few weeks earlier and explained what would eventually happen. They were enraged and surprised that I would be punished without ever having committed a crime. I told them that I didn't understand this indictment process either, but, that I would fight until the end to prove to them that I am completely innocent. As the FBI agents walk me out of the house, I keep my eyes glued to my daughters. I will never forget the tears running down their faces. One of the parents whose child slept over, is getting out of her car while I'm being forced into the back seat of one of the FBI's cars. It is utterly humiliating. This kids mom is going to think I'm the mistress of some drug lord. My heart is pounding. I can barely breathe.

The drive to the FBI office in North Miami Beach has been a strange one. I am handcuffed sitting in the back seat of a car with one agent driving and another beside me. All the while I remain calm. Out of nowhere, there is this very strange calmness that suddenly comes upon me. There are no tears running down my face anymore, yet, I am still in shock. Perhaps, reality hasn't set in. We arrive at the FBI office where I realize all twenty of us who are part of my case were just indicted together. There she is, Griselda, sitting inside an office handcuffed to a railing on the wall. I haven't seen her in nearly four years. I am placed in a room with two other agents. I thought, Really? I need two FBI agents? Do they really think I'm going to run? They just picked up Pablo Escobar's mistress, right?

I watch as others begin to arrive, many of which I did not know or recognize. My ex-fiancé, Jacob, who was also indicted, passes in front of the office I was sitting in. I haven't seen him in a long time either. During this time, we are all being processed: DNA, fingerprints, and mugshots. I am now officially a criminal. At least in the eyes of the law.

After a few hours later and a throbbing headache, we are all being transported to the U.S. Marshal's office to be placed inside a cell. I am being driven by the same two agents that had taken me from my home. Again, handcuffed, sitting quietly in the back seat. I look up at the sky out the window and ask, God, are you with me? Suddenly, a large ADT Alarm Company van passes on my side with large words that read, "You're Protected." It is part of their slogan, but, it seems like my question has been answered. I am at peace, for now.

We arrive downtown at the Federal Detention Center. I begin to cry the moment that I hear the car stop. The unknown is so unsettling. Tears falling down my face like an old, leaking faucet. Shackles immediately placed on my feet, and around my waist before I am taken to a cell. As I am approaching the cell, I stop walking. I feel paralyzed. Fear had once more taken over. The image of my daughters faces resurfaces and leaves me in tears. I feel a sense of doom. Never before have I been so afraid, angry, and desperate. It's all these emotions mixed together tearing me up inside and not letting me think straight. It's my ego that has been badly bruised. Fear is in control now. I have taken a backseat.

A few minutes later, Griselda walks into the same cell I am placed in. She walks in as if she was waltzing onto a dance floor. Unlike me, she looks calm, confident, and completely in control. She sits a few feet from me. I put my head between my legs, trying to calm down. Don't do anything stupid, I reason. I imagine myself getting up and strangling her. She is chatting and cracking jokes the whole time, convincing the other women in our case that what was happening was one big circus act. She repeated over and over that we have nothing to worry about. Listening to her say that to them, reminds me of the many times she would tell me not to worry whenever I questioned her about the loans. It only infuriates me to hear her voice and how cynical she is to sit here and lie this way. The sight of her only angers me even more.

So here we are sitting in the same damn cell. If I could manage to embrace every experience with peace in my heart, perhaps I could feel more at ease. Instead, I am drowning in fear, snot, and tears. One guard brings over a small rectangular box. Inside there is an apple juice and some disgusting bologna with two slices of bread. I am not hungry. The last thing I give a shit about is food right now. One girl in here asks me for it. She said if I wasn't going to eat it, can she have it? I watch her eating it as if it was a meal from Joe's Stone Crab. The guards return to get us, throwing shackles on the floor. They use them to escort us to the courtroom. At first, I feel liberated to be leaving the cold, gray cell. I refuse to use the toilet, which is out in the open where everyone can see. My bladder is full and sore, but, I grit my teeth and remain quiet holding my need to urinate.

The guard finally calls my name, I begin to tremble. I approach him hesitantly. He already has the shackles in his hands ready for me. Panic is taking over, my teeth, hands, and legs tremble at the sight of the chains. He is a tall, Hispanic looking man. I'm assuming he is Cuban. He tells me to relax; he isn't going to put them on tight. I begin to weep, feeling humiliated and belittled. Never in a million years would I have imagined I'd be in jail shacked from my waist all the way down to my ankles. I am no angel, but I've never been involved in any type of illegal activity. But today, though, none of that matters. I am a criminal to the system. After a lot of difficulty walking to the elevator, I am told to face the elevator walls. I could barely walk with the shackles weighing down my feet. They secure the chain around our waists, which connect to our hands and feet too. Where on Earth could we run to? It all feels so unnecessary. Their intent is to break us and, at least with me, they are accomplishing that. Kudos to them for reaching their goal. As I am riding on the elevator, all I could look forward to is seeing Vamp, my parents, and my attorney inside the courtroom. I am afraid I am being accused of a crime I have not committed, and I am scared that my word will not count.

We all sit down inside the cold courtroom. Walls are all covered in wood. Each of us are seated next to the other, shackled from our feet to our waist and wrists. I can't move. I hate not being able to move. My attorney, Susan approaches me and asks, "how are you holding up?" I respond with tears and choke up that I want to get out of here. She immediately asks if I have another $10,000 to give her so she could represent me today. I can't believe what I am hearing, at that moment. I feel like I am back inside the nightmare. Her careless question jabs my very soul, I feel so pained by how heartless she is about all of this. She never did any legal work for me. I was referred to her by Clay, my real estate civil attorney whom had been working on this case for nearly four years prior to my indictment. Clay thought I should hire a federal attorney for my case even after the fact, in civil court, a judge had already granted me that I was a victim of fraud and identity theft. My identity had been used by Griselda without my permission. How dare she demand this from me now? She hasn't defended me in court or met with the prosecutor whatsoever, yet, she is demanding $10,000 in addition to the $10,000 I already paid just to retain her.

Before I could speak, she continues, "I'm sorry, I won't be able to represent you if you cannot pay me at this very moment, but, you'll be fine. I will have someone else do it." She clacked away in her heels as I returned to my seat gasping for air without a chance to respond to her because I was all choked up. My legs trembling; what I just heard was frightening. I hired her to be my savior, the one who can get me out of this mess and now she is ditching me. My attorney has just dumped me in the courtroom without even giving me a chance to speak. Can't she see I'm falling apart here? What a heartless bitch.

My parents and Vamp enter the courtroom. I immediately feel better. I feel safe for only an instant. My friend Christina arrives with her friend, Alex, a bondsman just in case we need him to bail me out. As she waves at me, she is escorted out. No one is allowed to waive at the defendants or you are basically kicked out. Again, I panic silently. I have no attorney, and no Christina to support me. I am certain I will be left in jail to rot.

Griselda goes up first. She remains calm. The prosecutor's face is familiar but not because I have seen him before in this lifetime. I am certain that he and I have met a long, long time ago in another life. I feel this strange familiarity between us the moment he walks into the courtroom. I just knew he was the prosecutor. He is a tall, attractive, olive-skinned man. He almost looks like he's of Moors descent. Somehow, I feel we have a crazy

142

connection between us and recognize immediately that whatever we were in a previous lifetime, we weren't exactly best friends. It's so weird. I have never seen this man before or even felt this with anyone else. His name is Roger Cruz. He walks into the courtroom following twenty or more attorneys who represent the rest of us. For some reason, the moment he walks in, I spot him. I look at this man whom I've never seen before in my life and whisper to myself, Oh God, I know you, but not from here.

The prosecutor begins describing the case to the judge. This is when I first become aware of the extent of the case. He claims that we were all involved in a $40 million bank fraud and Griselda is the mastermind behind it. At the sound of $40 million, I almost throw up on my shackles. I am so screwed, is all I can think of. He mentions some money that had been traced from Griselda to a family member; it was, if I heard correctly, something like $200,000. Again, I almost throw up all over my clothes. How on Earth could I even be a part of this shit? I'm just finding out all of this crap. I begin to pray in silence throughout the entire hearing. Soon after, I hear my name being called up to the stand, my prayers tripled.

The prosecutor tells the judge that I was involved in conspiracy. I was being charged, at the time, with three counts: conspiracy to commit bank fraud, bank fraud, and accepting gifts. I'm baffled. What the hell is he talking about? These three charges are ridiculous. What part did he miss that all of my signatures had been forged by Griselda? Did he not get the memo? Did he not see that we went after the bank and filed for identity theft the moment we found out about the fraud? What the hell is going on here? Why is he accusing me of crimes I did not commit, without legal representation, and with very little understanding of what is going on. I begin to approach the podium, I can barely walk with all these shackles around my ankles, I almost fall to the ground as I am walking, the judge asks me who is my attorney. In tears, I respond I do not have an attorney, she has just left me here. She walked out of the courtroom. Suddenly, Steven Kassner stands up and shakes my handcuffed hands, announcing that he will now be representing me. Susan, the coldhearted bitch that had just dumped me, had given him my case. I guess they are colleagues. I just hope he's not an ass like she is. A rush of relief comes over me. I do not know who Steven is nor do I give a damn at this moment. I just want legal representation and someone to get me out of these chains. I can barely understand anything the judge is saying. She reminds me of a scene from Scooby Doo where Scooby is talking to Shaggy and it sounds like he's mumbling. My mind is all foggy. Great, she is letting me go on a personal surety bond of $200,000, which my parents will be signing. Soon after, we are all escorted back to the cold, grey cell before being released. I hear a guard calling my name as I'm walking past the door. He is telling me

I haven't been processed. He needs to take my fingerprints again. I'm shaking and still crying. I almost tripped walking towards him. The shackles weigh on my body and I feel totally depleted. I haven't eaten anything all day. It's now around 5:00 pm already. He asks me why I'm crying, and I respond, "I know you've probably heard this before, but I'm innocent." He smiles and says, "Well then, get yourself a good attorney."

He lets everyone else go back to the cell except me. He asks me to wait alone in a room. I'm confused. I don't know what to expect. I can't figure out why he is putting me in here by myself. Are they going to rape me? Holy shit, that's why he asked me to stay in this room by myself. You know, like you see in some movies. I'm sitting on a bench inside this little room wondering what is going to happen to me. After a few minutes, he opens the door and asks me if I want to go home. I respond in a hushed tone, "yes." He replies, "Well, let's go." He removes the shackles, returns my belongings, and walks me outside the doors. I'm the first one to be released. Was this an angel sent from the heavens or something? Thank you, God.

My parents are waiting for me, we hug and cry a little. I approach Jacob's girlfriend and reassure her that he is okay and he will be out soon. As we walk out of the building, my head begins to throb. I have a splitting headache and unbearable nausea. As soon as I get to the car, I look for a bag of some sort and vomit uncontrollably inside it. I

145

feel relieved. It is over. For now, the nightmare has ended.

It's 6:30 am, I have to get up and go to the office. I can't stay home and run the horror movie of yesterday's events through my mind. I have work to do. I have two psychologists who are here from Venezuela for a hypnosis course they came to take with me. Regardless of how I feel, my commitment today is to them. My kids and parents think I'm nuts for going to work today, but, I have a commitment and my issues are not the priority at this moment. Besides, what will I gain by staying home and replaying the scenes in my mind? I rather get up and distract myself with work.

It's been a tough few days. Not many of my friends know that I had just experienced one of the toughest days in my life. Some did call to tell me they read about it in the Miami Herald, while others, saw it on the news. Great, I'm famous now. I throw myself into work, as I have done so many times before. At work, I feel whole and at peace. There's definitely something magical about being in a profession where I'm committed to helping others. It gives me a reason to get up in the morning when all I want to do is stay in bed and just cry over what I just went through.

Whenever I am home watching TV and hear a knock at the door, all the fear and anxiety returns, even if for just a few seconds. I am consistently brought back to the day I was indicted. Loud noises begin to startle me like never before. I'm emotional often, but I try keeping it together somehow. I'm definitely concerned for my family. I often wonder what would be of them if something happens to me. I have been the provider, problem solver, savior, and Wonder Woman for all of them. I wear my costume proudly and well.

Since the past few weeks following my arrest, all I want to do is go to work and not think of anything else. I fear that if I stop to deal with what I'm feeling, I will break down. I don't have time to break down. I need a vacation, but, I can't travel. They made me turn in my passport the very next day after my indictment.

The last trip I took was just one month before the indictment. I had spent almost a month between Thailand and Cambodia. It was an amazing experience. I brought back the richness of that culture; the humility of the people. To think if things don't go well for me, that may be the last trip I will be taking for a long time. I can't imagine that happening. Travel is my reboot. I can't be without it for too long.

During the past few months after the indictment, I desperately try to keep the balance inside me. Vamp is always here to offer support. Leon has been trying to help me see that I am strong and that I could still win this. I try living a normal life, continue to spend plenty of time with the kids, my parents and friends, as usual.

147

I'm going out with a few friends tonight to Hillstone. I need to distract my mind. Who is that guy? I ask one of my friends. She has no clue, but, agrees that he is darn cute. His gorgeous green eyes catch my attention. He has salt and pepper hair, dresses very nicely, and has a warm, inviting personality. This hunk happens to be the spokesperson for the MDPD and also the person behind many of the films and reality shows filmed in Miami. Even so, I have never seen him on TV. Seems I caught his attention too, because he can't stop staring. He gets closer to where I'm sitting by the bar with my friends. He 'accidently' touches my leg while trying to order a drink from the bartender and immediately, apologizes. We connect eyes and smile. He then proceeds to ask me my name. His name is Robert.

Robert and I begin seeing each other. I feel strangely familiar and safe with him. I've dated occasionally, but nothing that really caught my attention. When it came to finding a mate, I'm a little too picky and a bit analytical for my own good. After all, I have a busy life and I don't have time to waste, or so I think. He is going through some stuff with his mother, who is very ill. I am going through my own stuff, too. It works perfectly.

A few weeks into dating him, I decide to fess up. I have to tell him what is happening. I have to come clean. While I'm over at his house one evening, I tell him that I've been indicted. Before he could speak, I explain the entire story from beginning to end. He's sitting across from me with his legs up on the sofa, listening attentively. Suddenly, he excuses himself and goes to the bathroom for what seems like a lifetime. He finally comes out, comes over to where I'm sitting, kisses me on the lips, grabs my hands, hugs me, and whispers in my ear, "Let's go to bed." I think it's strange, but, I can't resist the invitation; being in his arms feels so damn delicious. There are moments that I close my eyes and it just feels so good to be held by him. Then reality hits.

The next morning, after we exchange a few jokes and made love passionately, he sits across from me and frowns. He explains that he felt nauseous the night before when I told him that I had been indicted. He had sat in the bathroom, lifted the toilet seat, and clutched his stomach in awe. As I listen, I can't understand how my story could cause such a reaction, especially to someone who had been an undercover detective for so many years of his career. He then explains that he feels that way, because he could not be with me any longer. I am a felon. I am being convicted of a crime, and his profession would never allow him to have a relationship with a felon.

I can't believe what I'm hearing. A feeling of shock and anger takes over. I refuse to believe that these charges are keeping me from the first interesting connection I've had in a long time. My pride immediately kicks in. I respond curtly, "It's fine. I wouldn't want to jeopardize your career." I begin to remove the sheets from on top of me.

He tries to calm me down, explaining that he would try to fix this. He tells me that I didn't have to make any decisions for him, that he was a big boy. I continue to assert that there was nothing to do, that I wasn't going to affect him, so I quickly get out of bed, get dressed, and kiss him goodbye. I bolt out the front door feeling angry because of all the frustration raging inside me. How could these charges affect me in this way? Wasn't it enough that I had gone through the indictment back in September? Now I have to let go of someone I was actually interested in? What are the odds that I would even find myself involved with someone who represented the law? The irony of life.

My last relationship had been with an attorney. It has been a while since I was drawn to anyone, until I met Robert. So much for that, this shit is ruining everything in my life.

Chapter 7

June 2003

She is walking inside my office six months pregnant. Her dark hair pinned back, wearing a pair of black pants, a loose top, and a large purse. A man follows closely behind, accompanying her. It's her husband. She noticed the sign outside my office that read, 'Unconscious Creations Hypnosis.' She walks up to the front and places her hands in her pockets, "Hi, I'm Griselda, I'd like to try hypnosis."

I had just moved to my new office a few months earlier. Her mortgage broker's office is located across the street from my office, in a shopping plaza. She says she had seen the sign and wanted to know if I could help her with stress. She explains that being pregnant with her second child is making her feel hugely overwhelmed and emotional. Her oldest daughter is two-years old. I hand her my business card and quickly schedule an appointment. "I'll see you next week", I tell her as she slips out of the front door with a smile on her face.

During her consultation, I ask her a series of questions, including her childhood history, current issues she was struggling with, and her perceived stressors. After our first meeting, she eagerly schedules another session. "I'd like to start seeing you every week, because I'm very stressed" she confesses.

During our sessions, I use relaxation techniques, hypnosis, and coaching to help alleviate her stress and anxiety. She enjoys telling me stories of her earlier years and about some of her fears and insecurities. Typically, this was something everyone comfortably discussed after rapport was established. It is a normal mechanism of any human being to feel the need to express themselves after establishing a sense of trust. With time, we begin to develop a friendly bond with each other. She always expresses a great deal of appreciation towards my work and admires my dedication. Sometimes, she drops by my office just to chat; not discussing any of the issues at hand, mostly everyday talk. The kind of talk you have with a friend who visits you. We share a common ground and love for spirituality and kabbalah. Sometimes we get into conversations about known authors such as Michael Berg and Brian Weiss.

Time goes by and our relationship grows closer. Roughly a year later, my business continues to grow, and I move my office to a larger space with several rooms and she follows. She continues seeing me as a client, and, has also grown in her mortgage business. Recently, she has been experiencing some conflicts in her marriage. Her stress and concern have resurfaced again. I continue to see her, trying to help her manage her emotions. She always seems like an honest and trustworthy person who enjoys helping others unconditionally.

One afternoon she walked in with a Paulo Coelho book in her hand and asked me if I had read it, I respond "Yes, I've read The Alchemist," I retort excitedly. She insists I must read all his books; he was one of her favorite authors. Coelho was a very recognized spiritual-fictional writer. She is certain I'd enjoy them. One week later, a package arrives to my office. Inside are all of Coelho's published books - every last one.

This is just the beginning of her many gifts. By now, she is seeing me every other week. It isn't of any surprise to see her donating items or money whenever I collect for the homeless. I've always had a heart for those less fortunate. A few times a year, I enjoy collecting toys for the children's hospital, canned foods, clothing and other items. Griselda is always willing to donate. She loves writing very large checks to any of the organizations I am partnering up with. I always admire her for her will to serve others. I'm assuming she must be very well off, considering the lavish lifestyle she has.

My office is a small, but, comfortable, definitely not lavish. It's newly renovated and it's perfect for what I need at the moment. There are two other therapists who joined me, Laraine and Norma. I like them both very much. They are both really amazing at their work. Laraine is a total badass in Regression Therapy and Norma, she handles all the weight loss and smoke cessation clients. No one is as good as her. My long-term relationship with Vamp recently came to an end, so, I am focused solely on improving my business. I'm still dealing with a badly shattered heart. Vamp and I parted ways right before my move here, and I only dream of growing big, like Griselda. She is very successful not only in business, but, in life. She has a huge heart. She travels to the Dominican Republic very often and is always willing to give to those less fortunate. There was one time I was collecting clothes for a woman who had arrived from Cuba on a raft five months pregnant. The first thought in my mind was to call Griselda. She responds immediately. A few hours later, a courier arrives with a check written for five hundred dollars she was donating to the woman.

Another time was during the tsunami in Asia in 2004. My office is collecting items and donations for the American Red Cross. After I phoned her, she sent me a courier with almost $800 cash. She also sent me boxes filled with things such as toothpaste, Tylenol, clothes, and bandaids. Several times a year, I enjoy filling a large box with donations of toiletries and medicine. As usual, Griselda sends her kind donations to my office I typically fill the entire box with the items I buy using the money she sends me. I admire her, thinking that someday, when my business becomes as successful as hers, I will do the same. After all, I have always loved philanthropy and dream of giving back to others at a much larger scale. Not only does she contribute large donations to causes I support, but she also continues sending me gifts - for my birthday, Mother's Day, and most holidays. On occasion, she shows up at my office with very expensive trinkets such as, Chanel sunglasses, a Dell Laptop and Clive Christian perfumes; plus, much more. I always argue with her when she sends me such extravagant gifts with one of her couriers. My relationship with her isn't based on material things. I always consider her a friend. She continually expresses deep appreciation for the services I render and the friendship we have established. I guess she simply loves expressing her gratitude through gifts.

I admire how attentive she is to her children's needs. I consider her to be a very loving and caring mother; one who is extremely overprotective and a wonderful provider. Shortly after, Griselda and her husband split up, she told me that she had left him because he had been stealing thousands of dollars from her business while she was pregnant with her second child. She claims she found that out while she was on maternity leave for the birth of their second child. Apparently, he was buying properties and an expensive RV under his sister's name with the money from her company. She appears to be heartbroken and I am here to comfort her, as any friend would.

Time has gone by. Almost two years has passed since I have moved to the office. By now, our friendship feels more solid, regardless of the fact that we do not share any time outside of the office together, other than a birthday for one of her daughter's, we never really did spend much social time. Though, we do speak often on the phone, mostly just saying hello and catching up. I recently got involved in a new relationship, with Jacob. He's been a lieutenant at the fire station for the past 20 years, and I am finally rising to the top at my business. I offer many courses, workshops, and I'm typically booked for appointments months at a time. I work six days a week, 10 to 12 hour days. I feel exultant, but, I haven't fully healed from my breakup with Vamp. Even though it's already been two years. It sometimes feels like it was yesterday. I have to move on. Vamp and I remain great friends. I have long pretended I have been over him, too afraid of confessing that I am still in love. I fear that if he knows, he'd distance himself in an attempt to let me heal. Instead, I hold on for dear life; I love and mourn him in silence while at the same time convincing myself I am ready to get involved in another relationship. After all, it has been some time since our breakup. Vamp too has just gotten involved with someone else, so it was the perfect time for me to distract my mind and numb my heart.

I meet Jacob at a barbeque over at a friend's house. I'm not here to meet anyone, but, he seems charming. As a matter of fact, there's this guy who has been hitting on me all afternoon. He's gone as far as to invite me out on his helicopter. What a douchebag! Jacob notices this and immediately comes to my rescue, or, so he thinks I need rescuing. He pretends he and I are a couple, so the guy leaves me alone. We exchange our phone numbers while we hang out in the pool. I'm feeling quite comfortable around him. He has two kids, a teenage girl and boy. They are great kids. He is a Lieutenant at the fire station. He is very smart, and I particularly like that he has an interest in spirituality. He doesn't know much about the topic, but, he is very interested in learning. He's asked me to recommend him a few books because he wants to start reading. It's now been about a month since we started dating. Jacob knows about my friendship with Vamp. Understandably, he does not approve. However, I have made it quite clear to him that no one comes between Vamp & I. I am constantly assuring Jacob that I have no feelings for Vamp. I'm not intentionally lying to Jacob, I'm looking for a way to convince myself out loud.

Not too far along into our relationship, I decide to travel to Europe with two of my good friends, Eddie and Manolo. Of course, I left Vamp in charge of watering my plants and feeding the fish at home while I'm gone. Vamp and I own a townhouse together, which I stayed with after we broke up. Vamp has always been such a gentleman. The kind of man that is completely selfless and caring. Our breakup tore me to pieces, even though I had been the one to initiate it. One evening while Vamp and I were still a couple, I threw one hell of a tantrum. I was disgruntled over some money he had earned from a kitchen remodel. Vamp had just started his interior design business, and we had been discussing marriage for a few years by then. He was waiting to finish the project to buy me an engagement ring. That particular night, he announced that the ring would have to wait. "I'm going to use the money to help my mother remodel her kitchen," he explained as we lay in bed watching TV. That's when it happened. I reacted the way most kids behave when their favorite toy is taken away: a hissy fit, a tantrum, an explosion. With great regret, I still remember exactly how it all played out.

I sat up angrily and told him to leave our home. "It's over," I barked. "I realize now you will never buy me the ring. You will never marry me. There is always something more important in the way." By the time I came to my senses a few weeks later, it was too late. Vamp never took me back. I was heartbroken. Shattered to pieces. None of my efforts to win him back worked.

So, in comes Jacob, a man who wants to share his life with me. The only problem is that he wants me only for himself. He is too possessive. The name Vamp can't even be mentioned, because Jacob throws fits like a five-year old. He's clearly as torn as I am, but, in a very different way. I can only imagine his pain and desperation; being in love with a woman who just can't leave her past behind. Even though, I try endlessly to convince him I have gotten over Vamp, my eyes probably tell a completely different story. I am still madly in love with the man I had lost. Vamp and I talk every day on the phone; he stops by my office two to three times a week. We have lunch or breakfast together all the time. All of this is happening behind Jacob's back. Even so, it feels natural and innocent. After all, I'm not romantically involved with Vamp, not physically anyhow. Deep in my heart I am still in love with him though, a truth I am hiding even from myself. It feels like I'm living a lie. I want to be in love with Jacob the way I am in love with Vamp, but, how do I force myself to do that? Jacob is a not a bad guy. He deserves to be loved. I know I feel love for him, but, I am not in love with him because my heart has another owner. It's also difficult to love him because he argues about Vamp all the time and it's such a wear and tear on our relationship.

After a few months, Jacob proposes to me. More like he bought me a beautiful princess cut two karat diamond ring and gave it to me. No getting down on one knee, but, I got my ring. I accepted, and we are engaged. I finally got the ring I have longed for. Unfortunately, I should have never said yes. Not because he wasn't a great guy, but, because my heart is already married to Vamp. My ego believes the ring meant someone wanted to marry me. I am engaged for the wrong reasons and I am desperately trying to convince myself that this is what I want. As the relationship with Jacob progresses, we decide that I would sell the townhouse I live in, but, still owned with Vamp.

Jacob and I could buy a much larger home together after we sell it. After all, he has two teenagers that stay with us every other weekend along with my two girls who live with us. Off we go on a new adventure to find a much larger home. Jacob wants a five-bedroom home. I think five rooms is a little too much but, considering our salaries and lifestyles, we could certainly afford it.

For several weeks, we go house hunting. It's dreadful. I want a house in South Miami, or Pinecrest, but Jacob insists we should stay in Kendall. Finally, after several weeks of searching, we find our dream home, or so we think. It is a very beautiful five-bedroom, two-car garage home with a large pool and yard. Large lot and it's renovated too. Immediately, I contact Griselda to begin our paperwork. I provide her with everything she requests. It's an exciting time for us. The house seems to be what we are looking for. My townhouse has been put up for sale. Fortunately, enough, the very first couple that came to see it, fell in love and put an offer on it. Everything seems to be moving along smoothly except for my relationship with Jacob, who remains increasingly jealous of Vamp. In an attempt to make the relationship work, I tell Jacob that I barely speak to Vamp. He knows I'm lying, but, even he pretends at times to believe me. Nonetheless, we are in the process of buying a bigger home and I figure that it could distract me from how incredibly unhappy I feel with Jacob. I can't deal with his insecurities over Vamp. He makes such a big deal out of everything. It drives me nuts, but, I remain focused on selling my home and the purchase of our new one, hoping that he will get over this nonsense sooner or later.

Griselda calls me one afternoon at the office. Jacob happens to be here with me. She is looking for someone who wants to invest in a few properties that are for sale. She explains, that wealthy Russians own four apartments in a very luxurious building in Sunny Isles and are looking to sell them at a very affordable price. She wants to see if I'm interested. She needs someone to buy it with her but use that person's credit since hers was tied to several other investments she owns at the time. She was looking for an investor. It was a no-brainer. The apartment is located in a wonderful neighborhood, on the twenty-first floor, with an ocean view, in a building that has been completely remodeled. She says one of the apartments is being sold for $170,000 but, was worth several hundred thousand dollars more. She offers to pay me $10,000 up front on the investment just as long as we would buy it together and sell it in a year's time. Griselda will make sure to find a renter and in one year, we could make significant profit on the investment.

At that moment, I thought this was a great opportunity. I figured that if we could not sell or rent the property, I could always keep it as a vacation home. I immediately agree. She asks if Jacob wants to invest as well. She had a second apartment for sale in the same building on another floor. I briefly tell him about it while talking to Griselda on the phone, I ask him for his social security number, so she could begin to run his credit and tell us if he is approved. I haven't even give him a chance to think about it. As usual, I'm being the control freak I've always been. I tell Jacob, this is going to be a great investment for our future. Shortly after the excitement, I ask Griselda about the house we are buying. The one we had just put under contract. "How will we qualify for another loan?" I asked. "Won't it affect our purchase?" She replied with a firm and confident. "No, of course not! Based on your incomes, you will qualify for both. No worries." Which later translated into, worry a lot because I'm just bull-shitting you and you are dumb enough to believe me. You are just about to make the worst decision of your life. Why not trust her? She was not only a friend, but also a very smart businesswoman. As I hang up the phone, I am thrilled by the decision we have just made. Jacob exclaimed, "we're crazy!" I hug him and think about how awesome it will be to own two apartments on the beach. "Life is just amazing" I think quietly. I'm not only buying the house of my dreams, I'm finally getting married, and I just invested in a great property.

Nearly two weeks later, Griselda calls me to let us know that our closing is taking place in a few hours. We couldn't believe it was so quick, we still hadn't sold my townhouse or finalized the new home we are buying. All of this is happening so quickly. We are also planning a trip to Argentina where my best friend Amy is getting married. I am caught by surprise with everything moving so fast. So much is happening at the same time. She says that Gustavo will be picking me up and driving me to Regions Bank. That way, since I have never been to that bank, I wouldn't have to worry or get lost driving there. She said he would be in the area and would do me the favor. Gustavo is a close friend of Griselda and a former client of mine whom I worked with for stress and anxiety a while back. Frankly, it sounds like a great idea. The fact that I don't have to drive through Miami traffic is a blessing. A few minutes later, he shows up at my office and drove me to the closing. He comes in with me to Regions Bank and accompanies me as I approach a bank representative sitting at her desk. He tells her I am here for a closing from Griselda's office.

The bank rep smiles as she's opening a folder with legal size papers. She asks us to take a seat and begins going through all of the documents. There are so many, all of them in such small print. She shows me where to sign, flipping each page over for me. "Okay, all done," she smiles again. I remember seeing the amount of the purchase price, $170,000. Frankly, that's all I care to see.

She closes the file and says good-bye. I ask her if she is going to give me my copies. She looks at Gustavo. Biting her lip, she says Griselda will give them to me. Gustavo also assures me that once they are all organized, Griselda will have the paperwork and I could get them from her whenever I like. "Don't worry, Griselda will have them at her office" he assures me. Nothing seems out of the ordinary at the moment. He is someone I know and after all, I am at a bank. To my knowledge, that's how a closing is performed. Besides, why doubt Griselda when she is my friend and my mortgage broker?

Shortly after, we say good-bye and Gustavo drops me back off at my office where I continue with the rest of my day. I don't get a chance to call Griselda because I was so busy that day, but, I made a mental note to do so. Roughly two days later, a courier arrives with my $10,000 check as Griselda promised. I don't see anything wrong with it. $10,000 for this type of investment is pennies for Griselda. She has already mentioned she owns over seven properties in Dade County. I know her to be a very successful broker and investor. Jacob also had his closing more or less in the same fashion as mine if I recall correctly. I could never remember if Gustavo drove him there or if he drove himself. Either way, he too received his $10,000 check for investing and we figured it would go down towards our closing costs.

Not more than a week or so later, we receive news that the sellers of the home we are purchasing are backing off from the sale. They have decided to divorce in the midst of some conflict. We recently had the house appraised and inspected. We are just a week away from closing. I can't believe this shit is happening to us now. We are just inches away from moving into the new house. What the hell is going on?

At the same time, my townhouse is being sold and we are in the process of waiting for the final steps from the buyers to close on the property. Griselda assures me not to worry. The attorney for the sellers have contacted her and they are returning our $6,000.00 deposit. At this point, Jacob and I are incredibly upset and stressed out. We are also just a few weeks away from our 10-day trip to Argentina for Amy's wedding. I am stressed at the fact that we now have to start looking for another home. I can't stand the house-hunting process. Jacob assures me he will go see some of the houses and if he finds something he thinks I'd love, we'll go see it together. He knows how stressful this ia for me. I am so busy at work I don't have time to go back and begin the house hunting process all over again. Total bullshit.

My business is booming. I barely have time to eat lunch, let alone go see houses. The last thing on my mind is buying a house, but, inevitably we have to or we will be homeless soon. We wake up early today, and, go see a house that is located on a cul-de-sac. It's a lovely home that seems to fit the description of what we are searching for. It has a nice vaulted ceiling, located in a great neighborhood. It has a pool, five bedrooms, just like we want, a double car garage and a newly installed screened porch with a large yard and the house is beautifully landscaped. What more could we want? Even the layout of the house is perfect, yet somehow, deep down inside, I have this weary feeling. Maybe it has something to do with the fact that I had already fallen in love with the other property that fell through. Or maybe, just maybe, it's my intuition speaking to me and I fail to recognize that there might be danger ahead. Something in the pit of my stomach feels off. I have no clue what, but, I just don't feel happy. It could also be the fact that Jacob and I argue constantly about Vamp. His jealousy and insecurities grow stronger and it is debilitated every inch of our already wounded relationship. I called the engagement off three months after getting engaged and sending out the save the dates. It just doesn't make sense anymore to get married. We have too many issues over Vamp and I'm not willing to negotiate anymore. I have so much going on in my business that I don't have much time or interest to devote to the issues in my relationship with him. It feels like babysitting most of the time. Maybe I'm being unreasonable, or, perhaps, I'm even being a selfish bitch. I don't know anymore, and I don't have the time to invest in it either. My business is my only priority. I'm finally at a place where I'm thriving. I can barely handle the workload, but, I love it. I am helping hundreds of people reach their goals and overcome lifelong issues. I feel I have a purpose. The issues with Jacob are not important right now. We just need to find a damn home, so I can go back to being focused on work and move on with this already.

We discuss the purchase and after seeing how enamored he was with the house, I agreed. We contact Griselda to give her the news. Jacob does not force me to agree, he even suggested that we stop looking for homes and rent but I refuse. I am selling my home and I'm not going to rent a property that isn't my own. My ego is talking at the moment. So, we decided to go with it. Again, I ask Griselda if it would be fine with the bank now that we owned the two apartments. She assures me once again that I have nothing to worry about, the bank would approve it, we have already been approved for a $700,000 loan and therefore, we would be alright buying the house. We are relieved and excited that the house-hunting chore has come to an end. We are ready to put an offer.

Jacob and I are a bit worried because we haven't closed on my home, and the buyers keep asking for extensions. All the signs are there, but, my tenacious nature keep us going forward. After several days and extensions filed by my buyers, we are finally closing on my property. It's now about a week away from our trip to Argentina where I'm travelling with Jacob and my parents. Griselda will soon be leaving on her own vacation, so, we are trying to rush everything. She just phoned me to tell me that we are ready to close on the new home we are buying. Everything seems to be ready except one minor detail. In retrospect, I realize it was a major detail.

Jacob and I arrive at the closing, no one is here yet. Griselda asks us to arrive 15 minutes before the seller and title company. This looked nothing like the closing I experienced at Regions Bank. She explains that there was a little situation she encountered while preparing our closing statements. She found some minor setbacks with the bank. According to her story, she had to ask her aunt Fatima to be added to the loan in order to qualify us. Jacob and I look at each other with confusion written all over our faces. Something doesn't sound right, I remind her that she had assured me numerous times that we had qualified for the loan, she insist we don't have to worry about anything; her aunt knows I am an honest and responsible person. I don't know what to say at this point. My mind is definitely racing, and I have that very uncomfortable feeling again in the pit of my stomach. I don't understand how this closing process even works. She states that it is something common that happens with banks at the time of a closing and that it is totally legal. Caught somewhere between shock and puzzlement, all I remember saying was "Griselda, is this ok? Are you sure this is legal? If so, please tell your aunt not to worry. We will never make any late payments. Jacob asks if we are still the owners of the property and on the loan." She replies with a firm, "yes, of course you are." She went as far as to say that after a couple of months of living in the house, she will re-submit the paperwork to the bank and remove her aunt from all the paperwork, so Jacob and I would be the only ones on the title. I'm now a bit more relieved when she says this. Once again, she assures us we have nothing to worry about, these hiccups happen in the mortgage world. Minutes later, the seller arrives, sits down, and seconds after that, Sylvia from the title company arrives too and we begin the closing.

At first, the unexpectancy of the news left me feeling dizzy, but I reasoned it anxiety and confusion more than anything else. We all begin to sign those tediously long legal documents, shake hands, and are handed the keys to the property. Griselda gives the seller what seems to be a cashier's check. Jacob and I stay with Griselda and the owner of the title company after the seller leaves to hang out for a little while, when all of a sudden, she pulls out a briefcase full of cash. It looks like a scene from Scarface. Jacob and I don't understand what the hell is going on. Griselda sorts the money inside the briefcase. I look at Jacob with a what the hell face? She begins to tear up some documents on her desk and makes a few jokes to the other people in the room. I'm just watching in awe wondering what is going on. She makes no mention about what she is doing. I go inside my purse looking for my checkbook to pay her for our closing costs.

As I start writing out the check, I ask her how much the closing fees amounted to. "How much do I owe you?" I ask. She immediately announces that we owe her nothing. She would give this to us as our "wedding gift." Jacob and I refuse to accept the so-called gift, telling her she was crazy. We go back and forth arguing for several minutes. She insists in a firm voice, telling us we could not do this to her. It is a wedding gift. She mentions she will tear up any check we make out to her. Even so, I hand her a signed check and ask her to please fill in the amount we owe her, we want to pay for our closing fees. She grabs the check, rips it in half, and threatens to rip any other check I write to her. She tells us we have to accept her gift or we would offend her. She says that she wanted to take care of it herself. She had it planned out this way as a surprise.

Embarrassed by the gift, and after arguing for more than half an hour about this, we accept, and say our goodbyes. We walk away feeling hugely excited about our newly purchased home and very confused at how all of this just went down, but we trusted that she knows what she is doing since she is the expert. Jacob and I agree that she is very unorthodox in her ways and continue to focus on the fact, we could travel the next day to Argentina without any stress. During the next few months, we continue to focus on small projects, renovating a few things I wanted to change in the home and buying new furniture as we settle in. It's not long after, I start to develop some form of respiratory problem. There are nights where I can barely breathe. We just had the AC checked out and cleaned the ducts in each room, but, my breathing problems persist. I'm getting acupuncture and trying all sorts of holistic remedies. Nothing seems to work; I'm getting worse. My health is deteriorating. I've even had to call the paramedics a few times because there are times I can't catch my breath and I panic. Ironically, Jacob's a paramedic so he isn't too fond of me calling the paramedics when he is at work.

I'm finally going to see a specialist. The Pulmonologist diagnoses me with COPD, short for Chronic Obstructive Pulmonary Disease. The name alone sounds very serious. I went on to research it. Most of the stuff I've read, so far, says the symptoms worsen with time. There is no end to my misery. I am feeling awful and no matter what I do, nothing seems to improve my condition. Instead of taking any of the meds the doctor prescribes, I opt for a more holistic approach. I'm not in favor of prescription medication. The improvement is minor and there are nights I simply can't sleep. My breathing deteriorates with each passing day, and with it, my relationship with Jacob is also suffocating me. He can't leave the Vamp conversations behind us, not even now that we have bought a home together. I feel trapped and yet, when I'm at my office, I am free.

He's become so crippled by his insecurities, that just the sound of Vamp's name, sends him into a blind rage. Being in his presence has become unbearable. He finds any excuse to begin an argument, all of them relating back to Vamp. Many days I find myself lingering at work, hesitant to go home so I don't have to see his angry face. I know Jacob would be waiting for me, ready to raise hell. He has gotten into the habit of checking my T-Mobile account to see if Vamp and I have spoken. He's also started to hack into my emails to see if Vamp has emailed. While there is no justifying his behavior, in retrospect I can certainly understand why he feels so desperate. It must be devastating loving a woman who won't let go of her ex.

One morning, Jacob asks me to choose, "me or him?" Without hesitating, I say, "Him. It will always be him." I can still see the look of shock on Jacob's face. He is devastated, and with good reason. I continue, "he is my best friend, no one comes between us" For most, that would be the moment you leave the relationship. Not Jacob. He is just angry, bitter, and most importantly, hurt. What am I thinking? Or better yet, what is he thinking? At this moment, I think, how dare he ask this of me? I feel invaded and disrespected. I have made it clear from day one that Vamp would always be a part of my life. I've been open about what Vamp means to me. I did leave out a minor detail: that I was still madly in love with him. In spite of all this, I do not feel like I am in the wrong. I am defending my ego. I am standing up for the man I have loved for so long without any regard for the man that is standing before me. I am in the wrong. Even though, I do not acknowledge this in the moment. Jacob does not deserve this. Regardless of how crazy his insecurities are driving me, he deserves better. He is equally frustrated. The intensity of his love is too overbearing, it is smothering. It has gotten to the point that his love for me is no longer a healthy love, it is toxic. Months of turbulence pass, some better than others. The better ones are becoming more and more fleeting. Our only real arguments always come back to Vamp.

It's now been a few months since we purchased our home, we are in May of 2008. I just received a phone call from Griselda. She wants to meet with Jacob and I at my office as soon as possible. She sounds stressed. A few days later, I arrange it. During said meeting, she expresses some concerns she has with the real estate market. She discusses how her business is not doing so well. This is the beginning of the real estate crash. Jacob and I didn't think much of it. We hear in the news about some pitfalls in the market, but, we don't know how we can be affected by it. She explains that we need to decide if we want to sell the apartments or keep them rented.

It has been a year since we had purchased them. She insists that, at this time, we wouldn't profit as much as we'd anticipated, so, we could do with the apartments whatever we pleased. She brought up the point of short selling in the event we decide to sell but can't find a seller in time. I have no idea what that is, so, she went on to explain. A short sale is a sale of real estate in which the net proceeds from selling the property will fall short of the debts secured by liens against the property. That's when I take the opportunity to remind her that I never received the copies of my closing documents for the apartment. I explain that at the closing at Regions Bank, I was told she would have the documents. Griselda assures me that she will send them all to me in a few days. We end our meeting discussing a trip she will soon take with her kids to the Dominican Republic and Jacob and I will discuss and decide what we should do with the apartments. After all, if we couldn't sell them for the amount we wanted, we could always keep them as vacation homes.

A few days later, I have yet to receive the closing documents. I email her a short reminder. A few days after that, I still have not received an answer. I call and leave a few messages on her voicemail. Jacob and I assume she has already left for her vacation in Dominican Republic and that is why she hasn't gotten back to us. We decide we want to sell one of the apartments and keep the other as a vacation home, or perhaps a rental property. We agree to go to the bank today and request our closing documents we never got from Griselda. When we arrive at Regions, we saunter over to a bank representative, hand her our IDs, and sit down to wait. We had just explained to her that we had both had a closing here a year earlier, but, we never received copies of the documents.

I explain that our mortgage broker had them, but, I was having trouble getting a hold of her, so, we figured we'd come to the bank and request them ourselves. A few seconds later, while she types in my social security number on her computer, a page displays with a sentence that reads - "Fraud Investigation." My eyes widen in surprise and my jaw drops in panic. The lady looks at us while apologizing, "I cannot give you any information." Instead, she hands us a business card with the name and number of an investigator from the Fraud Task Force.

My immediate response is that there must be a mistake. I tell her that whatever the account says, was impossible; I want to see the branch manager at once. She calls the branch manager who proceeds to look up Jacob's information too. He types in his social and the same message appears on the screen, his account was under fraud alert as well. We demand an explanation, but, none is forthcoming. We ask to speak to someone higher-up but our request is denied. Our only instruction is to contact the task force investigator on the business card that was just handed to us. My legs tremble, my hands sweat like a waterfall, and my breath shortens. Jacob appalled and confused looks at me with his mouth open and no words are coming out.

We immediately phone Griselda multiple times only to get her voicemail. I leave numerous messages. We don't know what to do. We are desperate. My only thought is that this must be a mistake. I can't put the pieces together at this point. It hasn't crossed my mind that Griselda was committing bank fraud. If so, how would we even be involved? Our heads are racing with confusion and frustration.

We begin calling friends in hopes of being referred to a real estate attorney. We don't know what all this is about and are afraid of saying the wrong thing. The hunt for an attorney begins. We went to speak to three attorneys none would take the case. Finally, the fourth attorney, Clay, said he could help us and we retained him. He will look into the case and call the investigator himself. Still, I don't have my closing statements; all I have is our story. Griselda is nowhere to be found.

He calls us a few days later, eager to meet us. He has some very important information he's gathered. We rush to his office. We also have some news to give him. Griselda had finally contacted me. She claims to have been in the Dominican Republic when I questioned her about what was happening. She rushes off the phone, telling me to jot down her new number, I got rid of my old phone, she says. She tells me not to worry, this is a misunderstanding with the bank manager. She ends the call with instructions, "if anyone asks, tell them we never spoke. I can't understand why she is asking me to lie for her. I insist she tells me what is happening. Again, she tells me not to worry, that everything is fine. She insists that it was all a glitch in the bank. "She is taking care of everything", she responds. She doesn't sound nervous or freaked out. She is rather calm. I do not mention to her that Jacob and I have hired an attorney to look into this further. Quite honestly, she doesn't even give me the chance to, we hang up the call so quickly. She seems to be in a hurry.

We arrive at Clay's office around noon. We sit in the conference room; my stomach is turning. He lays out two files filled with copies his assistant just printed. He asks us to review them and place a stack of colorful post it notes on top; they are the closing statements on both of our properties. Clay says for us to place a Post-it Note on any documents we never signed. I am a bit baffled at his request. Why is he asking us to do that? I thought these are our closing documents.

As we flip through the pages, I notice that my signature has been forged on the majority of the documents. What the hell is this? Jacob recognizes his signatures have also been forged on several pages. The attorney asks us to go back and review all the documents once again to make sure we did not miss anything. We immediately reply, "why are our signatures forged on these documents." I'm so confused. I don't understand what is happening. I can't think of who would forge my signatures on these documents. He goes on to explain, that Griselda had forged our signatures on the closing statements. Even worse, she had taken out a line of credit worth over $300,000 on my property, and over $400,000 on Jacob's apartment. I still can't understand what he is saying. I shake my head in disagreement and firmly tell him that this is impossible; that Griselda was my friend and she couldn't have done that. I defend her with all my might, explaining that she was a good person, and we had been friends for many years. I'm angry at him for daring to say those things about her.

Jacob immediately interrupts and shouts, that I am blind. He is angry and blames me because she was my friend. The attorney understands exactly what had happened. I am in denial of perhaps the biggest betrayal of my life. To make matters worse, we also discover that she not only forged our signatures in obtaining these lines of credit, but, apparently there was a huge web of affairs now linked to our residential home. Her so-called 'aunt' who helped in obtaining our loan, wasn't her aunt, afterall. She is someone who is also linked to other lines of credit on other properties.

The attorney pulls up over six Quit-Claim Deeds that had been signed by what seems to have been Griselda, giving the property from Jacob to the aunt, the aunt to Jacob, Jacob to me, and so forth. It is so tangled up that I just can't make sense of it at this time. We are also told that there are roughly 187 to 300 loans involved, all done by Griselda. I begin to cry uncontrollably, feeling as if a dagger had just been driven into my back. Even at this moment, I continue to insist that there must be a mistake; it must have been someone else, but not Griselda. I just can't fathom her capable of such a thing. The worst isn't over yet. The attorney informs us that we are in trouble for purchasing the apartments and our residential homes with her. We are what they would later on allege to be, a straw buyer. A straw what? I've never heard of such a term. Little did I know, this is only the beginning of where all my lessons would soon begin.

Reflection

Many of us have experienced difficult challenges, such as illness, pain, or, the death of a loved one. This undoubtedly shifts and darkens our reference point. Given the severity of the problem, it's easy to think that God or whatever you believe in, has abandoned us. Rather than recognize the opportunity for growth, we victimize and blame ourselves. This creates a ripple effect, most of which are unstable and untrue. Creating a disconnect with our own selves and allowing fear to take over. A fear that cripples and doesn't allow us to see the blessings that are before us. Ask yourself, how does fear serve me? The more you think about it, the less likely you are to come up with a valid answer. You may even attempt to convince yourself that some fears are valid, such as the fear of dying. Yet, if you truly understood that your soul never dies, you would no longer fear death. If not death, you may fear the possibility of losing your job. The reality is that even if you should lose your job, you can find an even better job than the one you had before. The key is to change your perception.

You'll find that whatever your fears or challenges may be, they all represent a lack of unity and it derives from your ego. Rather than think upon fear, what if we tried identifying the root of those fears, by challenging them, then releasing the energy they carry to the best of our ability. I bet, we would likely gain the empowering realization that we are capable of dissolving all the barriers around us. Soon enough, we would unleash inner qualities that were dormant inside each of us. While this notion may seem somewhat difficult or even impossible for some, I'm certain that if we try it, our lives would radically change.

You are creating a perspective shift. You are aligning your thoughts intentionally, with the will of Love rather than Fear. Fulfillment can only occur when you are selfless and willing to share your love with others by forgiving what you believe they have caused. Even if you fear the idea of letting go. Sometimes, we lead ourselves into believing that letting go is a sign of weakness, when in fact, it is a sign of strength. It is only by letting go that we release what has been holding us back.

By becoming self-aware, and engaging in the selfless act of forgiveness, our emotions no longer dominate our thoughts from a place of fear. Once our thoughts are no longer chaotic, we stop attracting the same challenging, negative realities. We are freed of our limiting patterns.

There are many opportunities for us to learn about our own limitations. Personally, It was my desire to live as well as my longing for life that brought me back from the depths of myself. At first, I couldn't wrap my head around the idea that my circumstances were meant to catalyze personal growth. Slowly, I came to the realization that if I did not own my experiences today, I would continue to repeat them in order for me to learn the very lessons I was denying. Growth cannot be delayed or avoided.

Acknowledgements

A very special thank you to all who collaborated in the creation of this book. Mark, my amazing husband, thank you for helping me bring this book to fruition, your support and love is invaluable. Gemeny, my love, my daughter, you are truly brilliant. I'm grateful for having you push me to pour my heart into this book. Yesenia, I can't thank you enough for the many Monday's we got together to help me work on this book. Deborah, thank you for the countless hours you put into the first part of this manuscript, your help was invaluable. Rosalin, thank you for putting the time into transcribing my illegible handwritten manuscripts. To this day, I have no idea how you managed to decipher my prison letters!

I am very grateful to Dennise for her kind contribution. Coni, Laraine and all of those who were there for me during such difficult moments.

My deepest gratitude is to my friend, colleague, and brother from another mother, Todd. I truly could not have risen from the ashes without your support and friendship when I was first released from prison. Thank you for believing in me regardless of where our lives and friendship is today.

This is me at the age of 7, at the height of my Wonder Woman Complex. Little did I know how terribly that would serve me later in life.

About the Author
Sheena Eizmendiz

A published author of "Master Guide of Hypnotic Scripts: Hypnosis Made Easy," Sheena is a national corporate trainer and keynote speaker on the topics of stress, leadership, emotional intelligence and positive psychology. Sheena also specializes in working with top Fortune 500 companies by providing each employee with a personalized solution. She helps individuals stay free of personal distractions and remain more focused on the job through her corporate wellness trainings
Once deemed, the "Coaching Expert" by Miami's iHeart Radio's Y-100 Station for her weekly talk show. She has over 20 years working with an extensive client list including CEOs of multi-billion dollar companies and political leaders. She has appeared in numerous TV and radio stations throughout South Florida as a leading expert in her field. Her tools and techniques aim to bridge the gap between Clinical Hypnosis, Personal Development and Executive Coaching with Neuro-linguistic Programming (NLP). She is passionate about inspiring and instructing others on how to improve their lives and achieve their goals.

For more information, visit:
www.sheenaeizmendiz.com

$14.95
ISBN 978-0-9968446-0-4
51495>

9 780996 844604

186